Winning the
Knowledge
Game

'This is a great book. Knowledge is no longer presented as a commodity to be used in the pursuit of ends but as an enormously essentially part of the process of achievement. We are challenged to think outside our own paradigm, break through our safety nets in the pursuit of growth. Alastair's advice is personal yet strategic, straightforward yet full of depth.'

ANN BRASSIL, Director of BreastScreen, NSW

'Given Alastair Rylatt's previous books, I was expecting *Winning the Knowledge Game* to be an easy-to-read book on learning and knowledge with loads of practical tips, and this it certainly is. What I was not expecting is that his latest work is also crammed with valuable strategies for improving personal and organisational effectiveness. It should be compulsory reading for all MBA students, as well as managers and professionals in organisations, whether public or private sector, large or small.'

RODNEY GRAY, Principal of Employee Communication & Surveys, NSW

'In this future-world of information markets, businesses that fail to create a culture of knowledge and learning will not realise their potential. The managers with the courage to create an intelligent learning environment will win the knowledge game, benefiting their staff, themselves and the business.'

DR CHRIS RISSEL, Director, CSAHS Health Promotion Unit
& Editor In Chief, *Health Promotion Journal of Australia*

'*Winning the Knowledge Game* is not just for the knowledge junkies but is a thorough resource for both managers and staff in any organisation.'

KERRI SIATIRAS, Director, SWIM Ltd

'This comprehensive look at knowledge and its gathering, storage and use, contains a wealth of tips and techniques, examples, anecdotes and references as it guides the reader through the well-researched components.'

GRAHAM WARBURTON, Director, IT, Roche Products Pty Limited

Winning the
Knowledge
Game

A smarter strategy for better business
in Australia & New Zealand

ALASTAIR RYLATT

The **McGraw·Hill** Companies

Sydney New York San Francisco Auckland
Bangkok Bogotá Caracas Hong Kong
Kuala Lumpur Lisbon London Madrid
Mexico City Milan New Delhi San Juan
Seoul Singapore Taipei Toronto

 **Professional**

Text © 2003 Alistair Rylatt
Illustrations and design © 2003 McGraw-Hill Australia Pty Ltd
Additional owners of copyright are acknowledged on the Acknowledgments page.

National Library of Australia Cataloguing-in-Publication data:

Rylatt, Alistair, 1957– .
  Winning the knowledge game.

  Includes index.
  ISBN 0 074 71342 6.

1. Knowledge management. 2. Success in business. I. Title.

658.4038

Published in Australia by
McGraw-Hill Australia Pty Ltd
Level 2, 82 Waterloo Road, North Ryde NSW 2113
Acquisitions Editor: Javier Dopico
Production Editor: Rosemary McDonald
Editor: Ruth Mathieson
Proofreader: Tim Learner
Indexer: Diane Harriman
Designer (cover and interior): Jan Schmoeger/Designpoint
Typeset in 12/14 pt Bembo by Jan Schmoeger/Designpoint
Printed on 70 gsm bulky woodfree by Pantech Limited, Hong Kong.

The McGraw·Hill Companies

Contents

About the author

Alastair Rylatt is one of Australia's leading contemporary thinkers in modern business management and workplace learning. Alastair's mission is to inspire the spirit of learning, enlightenment and innovation in business. He is an inspiring presenter, expert strategist and award-winning author. His presenting and writing have taken him to major conferences and clients throughout the world.

Alastair holds a Bachelor of Business Degree and a Graduate Diploma of Employment Relations. He is a fellow of the Australian Institute of Training and Development and an Associate Fellow of the Australian Human Resources Institute.

Alastair has written a number of other books including *Learning Unlimited*, *Navigating the Frenzied World of Work* and *Creating Training Miracles*. *Creating Training Miracles*, which he co-wrote with Kevin Lohan, won the Best Business Book for the Asia Pacific in the Financial Times/Booz Allen and Hamilton Awards as well as reaching the global final in London in 1996.

Alastair has consulted to over two hundred organisations in a vast array of industries and businesses over fifteen years. Clients include the Australian Institute of Management, the City of Sydney Council, Coca-Cola, General Sekiyu KK (Japan), Roche Products, the Singapore Institute for Management and Vodafone to name a few.

Alastair Rylatt is the director of Alastair Rylatt Consulting, and he can be contacted at alastair@alastairrylatt.com or visit his Workplace Learning Help Desk at www.alastairrylatt.com.

Preface

Wonderful learning and innovation rarely happens by chance. Whether you are in a business or learning for yourself, you need the right game plan to succeed. Sometimes luck may come your way but, more often than not, it is your perseverance and smart thinking that matter most. The benefits of winning with knowledge can be far reaching, ranging from obvious gains such as improved profitability and performance through to other outcomes such as improved adaptability, better levels of service and an enhanced contribution to customers and society.

As a corporate consultant, speaker and manager for over 20 years, I have seen compelling evidence that long-term business success is clearly linked to how well we position our knowledge and build on each other's genius. In business, as in life, managers need to acquire a diverse and often complex range of skills to succeed. This message is particularly true for the challenge of winning the knowledge game.

People now live and operate in a business world where comparison, learning and competition play an essential part. Whether you are in a small business selling fruit and vegetables or you are a manager making sense of the latest advances in technology, such awareness and insight is vital. It seems that managers are now being judged on their level of *know-how*. In today's modern workplace there is nowhere to escape the need for knowledge. It is how fast we develop our capability and learning that is important.

One of the great challenges of modern business is not being fooled that you are learning smarter when you are using the latest palmtop or killer software application. The reality is that such tools and technologies are no guarantee that you are learning what you need to know.

The goal of this book is to pull together the very best advice and help you to improve your business and/or career success. It is my experience that most managers struggle to have the right conversations they need to help them move forward. They are often caught in a silo of similar thinking people or feel that they do not have the time or willpower to question their own assumptions and experience. As a result, protection of one's territory, identity and expertise takes precedence over building higher level know-how.

What makes this challenge difficult is that our talent can often be hard to see. The genius that creates breakthroughs, ideas and innovation may lie hidden in a clever design such as a microchip, a jingle or a new patent or simple procedure. Such cleverness needs to be drawn out if we are to succeed. To win the knowledge game we must be prepared to live and learn from talented people and encourage others to do the same. The benefits are plain to see, whether it is the freshness and taste of a meal, the quality of advice you receive from a lawyer, or how important you are made to feel when you first arrive at a hotel. Our knowledge and capabilities make the huge difference in how businesses and their customers perform and it must be nurtured and treasured. It is how we grow our imagination, enterprise and skill that is vital.

Throughout life, each person needs to perfect their own unique method of finding the tools, technologies and know-how they need to grow and develop. Those who succeed are those who nurture and build their capabilities on a regular and continual basis. Knowledge by its very nature is impermanent. What may one day seem groundbreaking and helpful may not be so the next. Learning is not something that can be bottled and kept forever; it is a living process full of twists, turns and new discoveries. The key is to see each moment in life as an opportunity to discover new insights, ideas and wisdom. With this attitude winning the knowledge game is almost guaranteed.

To help you achieve this goal this book provides the tips and knowledge you need to modify or improve your current approach. To do this, you will find out very quickly that this book gives you easy access to many fields including law, psychology, technology, management, marketing and accounting. The result is a stand-alone resource full of great tips, checklists and practical action.

Although the primary target audience for this book is managers, a host of other people can also benefit from this book. These include senior executives, team leaders, small business operators, trainers, human resource professionals, information technology specialists, intellectual property advisers, school principals, teachers, academics, librarians and students.

My biggest wish is that this book will help stimulate much higher levels of innovation through smarter teamwork, collaboration and the sharing of insight. We must all discover smarter ways to build better customer relationships, reputation and service delivery. Most people understand that to have smarter and better businesses, we need to enhance the spirit of learning, innovation and enlightenment. Winning the knowledge game is the path to success in the twenty-first century marketplace, and that means investing in our brains, ingenuity and know-how.

ALASTAIR RYLATT

Director, Alastair Rylatt Consulting

www.alastairrylatt.com

Acknowledgments

During the last two decades I have been lucky enough to travel to most corners of the globe and observe much about how people win or lose the knowledge game. In Australia and New Zealand there has been a host of people who have helped shape my thinking. In more recent years several of my clients such as Roche Products, CSIRO, the Office of State Revenue, St George Bank and Parramatta City Council have been marvellous. I especially would like to thank Gradipore for their help in providing some practicality to the topic of protecting intellectual property.

Additionally, there have been a number of professional associations that have provided me with many opportunities to expand my know-how. These include the Australian Institute of Management, the New Zealand Association for Training and Development, the Australian Institute for Training and Development, the Human Resources Institute of New Zealand, Standards Australia's Knowledge Management Network and the Australian Human Resources Institute.

On an individual level, Rudi Weber, Cec Pedersen, Karl Erik Sveiby, Rodney Gray, Tim Kannagieter, Glenn Capelli, Dr Francesco Sofo, John Davies, Frances Tweedy, Peter Marshall, Brent Stubbins, Geraldine Murphy, Megan Griffiths, Darryl Rubiolo, Eugene Fernandez, John Davies, Robert van der Spek, Harrison Owen, Laurel Draffen, Goran Carstedt, Robyn Hutchinson, Elliot Massie, Ronald Forbes, Professor Chris Hall, Peter Williams, Kevin Lohan, Robyn

Kramer, James Davidson, Kerri Siatiras, Javier Dopico, Pamela Dodd, Greg Schmidt, Sarah Heal and Marty Verry have all been very supportive to me on this journey.

Finally I would like to thank my wonderful wife Elaine, my best mate Peter (Selby) Jenkins and my brothers, Andrew, Dennis and Philip, for their love and guidance, and finally to my dear mum who sadly died only weeks before this book was completed. May your spirit of courage, endurance and laughter last forever.

To a world of great compassion, insight and shared advantage.

Introduction

The knowledge game

Learning through knowledge should be no stranger to us; we have accomplished this playing games as children or while perfecting new skills later in life. Business is also full of countless opportunities to build our capacity, agility and expertise. To a very large extent, business success is determined by how well we play these knowledge games and how well we understand the dynamics of being human.

Whether we are at home or work, 'winning the knowledge game' is a skill we cannot ignore. Irrespective of whether we like or dislike the games people play, it is very difficult to remain detached and unaffected by the need to interact with and learn from each other in solving life's challenges.

To be successful, contemporary business needs a knowledge game plan. Managers must encourage a business culture where ideas and talent can be built without unnecessary obstruction and interference. Knowledge is not something we can manage or box. It often has a personality all of its own, and it can grow, fade away and change without warning. Managers need to be wary of exerting too much control and command, and be more open to the benefits of teamwork, collaboration and sharing.

More often than not it is our capacity to inspire imagination, foster talent and put knowledge to work that makes our business stand apart from other businesses. As Laurence Prusak, an international authority on knowledge and innovation, says—the only thing that gives an organisation a competitive edge (i.e. the only thing that is sustainable) is what it knows. This includes how it uses what it knows, and how fast it can know something new.

As life has taught most of us, knowledge games by themselves do not necessarily generate benefits. We need to approach them with purpose, rules and intentions to reap the rewards. We have to be confident that we are deploying the right tactics and methods. Listed below are seven 'rules' of the 'knowledge game', which have not only helped me to succeed in games in the past, but I believe they have direct application to the world of business. To be successful in winning with knowledge we must:

1. be clear about what and why we are playing
2. understand the game rules, objectives and conditions
3. inspire ourselves and others to put in their best effort
4. where possible have a game plan, which builds on shared goals
5. learn as we go and position our knowledge
6. evaluate and compare our progress, and, if necessary, revise our strategy
7. apply what we have learnt for next time.

Of course these rules are no miracle cure. You must be prepared to stimulate fertile ground for innovation and performance improvement by searching out new insights, securing strong relationships and being courageous enough to build a plan of action.

In some cases your goal in winning the knowledge game may be about becoming the best, the first or even the largest. On other occasions you may be quite happy to build on the ideas of others and quietly innovate. Winning the knowledge game in business need not be played using a win–lose scenario. Increasingly, leading organisations find that pooling expertise even among traditional competitors is smart business. By doing so you increase the chance that everyone can win in an ever-changing world. Alternatively, your focus may be around the theme of greater contribution to society or enhancing customer value. Whatever your position or intention in business, each manager needs to respond smartly with the right tactics, tools or systems in order to succeed. This is particularly so when we do not know who is going to be our next critic, competitor or customer.

Playing with integrity

As you would expect ethics are vitally important to how we play the knowledge game. The opportunities for a manager to be unethical or unlawful when it comes to collecting, storing and acting on knowledge and intellectual property are enormous. In many situations people may be unaware that what they are doing could be deemed unlawful or unethical—for example, eavesdropping on a conversation between people from a competing business at an airport lounge. Would you call that unethical? Some people would say it is fair while others would say it is not. Such enquiry is central to how we play the knowledge game.

For many executives and managers winning the knowledge game is like fighting a war—that is, winning at any cost. They feel any action or business practice is acceptable, as long as the enemy is defeated. When I was discussing possible titles for this book, one publisher suggested 'Winning the Knowledge War'. I felt for many reasons— one being how the world has changed since 11 September 2001—that the war title was an untimely and bad taste choice. In war the rules are dramatically different. Espionage, misrepresentation, piracy, theft, bribery and covert surveillance are seen as fair game. I would argue this should not be the case in business, but I know there are many people who would disagree with me.

It is my view that winning in business can and should be undertaken in a more enlightened and transparent way. Sure, you may need to deploy counterintelligence measures, but this can be done in a spirit of fair play and the utmost integrity. We can create a business model that sees the game of knowledge as an exciting opportunity to achieve excellence and improve performance without resorting to unethical tricks or foul play. Most likely you will need a risk management strategy that helps protect your rights and know-how. This may mean taking direct legal action, safeguarding trade secrets or protecting intellectual property.

To help you build your own strategy for winning the knowledge game you may find the code of conduct of the Society of Competitive Intelligence Professionals (SCIP) at www.scip.org a useful starting point. SCIP suggests that you should consider the following:

Integrity:
– [Code of Conduct]

- continually strive to increase the ethical use of competitive intelligence
- comply with all applicable laws—domestic and international
- accurately disclose all relevant information including one's identity and organisation, prior to all interviews
- fully respect all requests for confidentiality of information
- avoid conflicts of interest in fulfilling one's duties
- provide honest and realistic recommendations and conclusions in the execution of one's duties
- promote this code of ethics within one's company, with third-party contractors and within the entire profession
- faithfully adhere to and abide by one's company policies, objectives and guidelines.

Without doubt, integrity is a quality that is priceless—particularly as excessive greed, golden handshakes and backroom deals gain more and more media attention and community backlash. The truth is that we may not be able to control the behaviour of others, but we can still be a leader of integrity and transparency. One simple way of testing our behaviour and choices is to consider the following scenario. How would you feel if what you are proposing to do is reported on a national current affairs television program? If you feel uncomfortable about how your intentions or dealings may be reported, it is most likely that your actions may be considered either unlawful and/or unethical. This simple 'gut test' is a useful guide to help you travel in the murky ground of competitive intelligence and ethical behaviour.

Structure of this book

Having introduced the theme of winning the knowledge game and the importance of integrity, let us now explore what is ahead. First of all, *Winning the Knowledge Game* explores three fundamental questions. In answering and exploring these questions you will be able to implement and sustain action in any business or career. These are:

1. How do we open our hearts and minds to learn smarter?
2. How do we grow competitive advantage?
3. How do we ensure lasting success?

Opening hearts and minds

Before implementing systems and changes in any business it is imperative that curiosity and commitment are engaged. It is here where most managers and change processes go wrong. To win the knowledge game we must first open people's hearts and minds to learning. Avoid making the common mistake of jumping into action before gaining the support of people. The first five chapters of this book explore a number of issues, including starting with a winning strategy, building trust, smarter thinking and learning, and finally nurturing meaningful conversations. It is recommended that you either read or skim through this first section. It seems most of the problems associated with winning the knowledge game are due to a failure to get the basics right, and it is these basics that are the focus of the first five chapters of this book.

Growing competitive advantage

In this part of *Winning the Knowledge Game* the second key question of how do we grow competitive advantage is answered. Here you will discover the latest tools, techniques and best practice approaches to improving your know-how, innovation and performance. Over eight chapters we will explore a diverse range of topics ranging from smart leadership, competitive intelligence, nurturing the change, better talent management, protecting intellectual property, reaping the benefits of digital technology, increasing customer loyalty and polishing your training performance. The goal of this second section is to help you to custom design your own personal and unique approach to knowledge and innovation in your business and career.

Ensuring lasting success

Winning the Knowledge Game ends with three chapters on the vital themes of evaluation, measurement and ongoing success. Here the primary focus is on helping you evaluate and measure know-how, genius and insight. This will be discussed in Chapters 14 and 15. Then in the final chapter on passing the final test, seven major themes that surfaced for me as I wrote this book are highlighted. There are also some concluding tips on better managing our thinking and brain power.

To help you gain the most out of this book, each chapter contains short pieces of insight rather than long-winded explanations. Checklists, examples and summaries are extensively used to make the application and choices easier. At the beginning of each chapter you will find five discoveries and at the end a short summary. At the end of the book there is a comprehensive reference section, which includes extensive Internet references. Also, where possible, Australian and New Zealand examples and quotes are shared without detracting from important worldwide case studies, research and observations.

May you enjoy the thrills and spills of winning the knowledge game for many years to come.

PART 1

Opening hearts and minds

Inspiring higher levels of curiosity and imagination is the major foundation for winning the knowledge game. Managers need to devote time and effort to winning the hearts and minds of people to the shared importance of building a smarter and more agile business.

There are many capabilities that help this pursuit. These include building a culture of discovery and innovation, sponsoring higher levels of trust and support, exploring new ways of expanding one's thinking, combining faster and deeper levels of learning, and being prepared to reinvigorate collaborations, teamwork and relationships.

These capabilities are the essential skills for twenty-first century business and personal growth. They are necessary in all forms of human interaction, whether managing a large organisation, a small business or a professional firm, or working for a not-for-profit organisation.

CHAPTER 1

Having a winning strategy

'In a post-industrial world, the only thing that counts in terms of whether you survive is not milk, it's not butter, it's not fruit, it's not oil, it's ideas.'—PROFESSOR FRANK CROWTHER

Having a winning strategy requires:

- knowing your business and positioning your knowledge
- creating a safe space for people to toss around ideas
- eliminating behaviour such as bullying, hoarding of information and backstabbing
- encouraging people to be intelligent together
- making it very clear why sharing is important.

Getting the basics right

Let us begin by asking two simple questions:

1. What makes a truly outstanding business?
2. What capabilities does a business generate that makes it extra-ordinary and very hard to copy?

These two questions are at the core of winning the knowledge game. Outstanding business performance begins and ends with the enduring ability to know your marketplace, position your knowledge and build your capability. No industry or business can ignore the fact that it must tailor its products and services to an increasingly sophisticated and aware audience, community and/or customer base. The best businesses are very clear about their purpose. They have built a compelling vision of their future and have created a practical plan for how to get there.

As one reads the literature, hears stories and observes practices, there is a real sense that *know-how* is the critical difference. Learning and knowledge can be transformational and groundbreaking. Whatever our trade, profession or passion, putting knowledge to work is central to everything we do. No one can ignore the fact that wisdom and higher levels of insight will set us apart from the rest. As Thomas Stewart (2001) says in his book *The Wealth of Knowledge*, 'knowledge is a rock'. Uniqueness, particularly unique knowledge, is where business wins or loses.

Here are six examples that will give you a feel for good practices in knowledge and innovation in a variety of industries:

1. The Australian Red Cross Blood Service created a team-based environment where informal networks and cross-functional groups share and collaborate. Staff are encouraged to think differently and to look at issues from an organisation-wide perspective.
2. Dunedin City Council's intranet—KnowledgeBase—enabled its call centre to resolve 78 per cent of calls immediately, without the need to refer to specialist staff. This application was developed in-house, and is now marketed by an external company. Dunedin City Council receives royalties for the sale of KnowledgeBase, which has now been implemented in 12 other local authorities.

3. Ford Motors introduced a knowledge exchange between thirty-seven plants around the world to reduce the time taken from the concept of a car to the marketplace. On the latest count 2800 proven practices were shared and the production cycle had been reduced from thirty-six to twenty-four months. The value of improvements is estimated at US$1.25 billion.

4. John Paul College, with the assistance of notebook computers, wireless networks and on-line learning technology, has become one of the largest schools in Queensland. Its vision of pioneering 'anywhere anytime' education has led to the establishment of a connected learning community involving collaboration with student teachers, parents and the wider community in learning and education.

5. Lgov NSW Learning began using webcam to do mentoring and coaching, and supplement skills training to local government managers in remote locations. The result is a higher level of learning and skill development.

6. At Westpac Institutional Bank computer desktop users source all relevant customer details while also detecting who else has been doing similar searches, leading to better cooperation and smarter thinking within the business. Advances in searching, mapping and understanding customer preferences aid ongoing improvements in customer yield and satisfaction.

As you think about these examples of varying complexity and size, it is easy to see that the potential and terrain for improving knowledge work and innovation is immense. As you would expect there are many factors that help create business value, such as enhancements in technology, better customer service, patenting a new product or the ability to cut transaction or production costs. These capabilities cut across the fabric of what drives outstanding business in most modern industries and occupations. With the right attitude and thinking, solid progress can be made.

So what generates a successful strategy? Generally, there needs to be a business leadership that nurtures trial and error as well as a neverending commitment to ingenuity and discovery. This needs to be backed up with a clear focus, strategies to engage motivation and then practical plans to build the right systems. There must be a clear realisation that winning the knowledge game has no miracle solutions and quick fix answers. One needs to be in the game for the long haul. Such intention and spirit is essential before the rewards can be reaped. Often there will be a slowdown in productivity and service before the benefits of learning begin to sink in. This can be seen in training courses where people need time and practice to develop their expertise before positive change can be seen.

Assuming we have the basic attitudes right we will need to work hard to stay in the knowledge zone. Businesses must first lead from the top to engender a corporate culture of neverending improvement. All the techniques, tools and technologies in the world will not make a scrap of difference if the heart of the business fails to champion daily innovation and continuous improvement. Being quietly comfortable and thinking that things can cruise along is a proven recipe for decline or stagnation. We must be prepared to look for new and better ways. We also need to be receptive to 'unlearning' what we know, while also being open to discovering what we do not know. It is vitally important that we test our assumptions, myths and taboos. In this fast-paced world it is very easy to miss the blatantly obvious, and so we must work hard to keep our antennas and radar operating. Business must be prepared to move beyond just doing tasks and completing projects. It must be prepared to take note of the learning that comes from experience. Life is a great teacher if only we take the trouble to learn the lessons that it provides us. At times managing such dynamics can be disturbing, unsettling and uncomfortable. Each business needs to feed off chaos, uncertainty and expediency to uncover what is most necessary and important.

Better practices in knowledge and innovation display a clear understanding of five guiding principles:

1. To be successful one must create a clear and inspiring vision for change, thereby assisting people to clearly understand why better knowledge is vital and why it is deeply important to everyone involved.

2. Leaders need to stimulate a spirit of collaboration and mutual advantage by sharing what they know, while learning what they do not know. Good leaders realise that knowledge cannot be conscripted or forced; it must be volunteered and encouraged.

3. Knowledge work is essentially a social experience. It needs exchange and interaction. Digital technology, tools and systems are a great help, but people are needed for it to work.
4. Knowledge is not about which talent you hire or the intellectual property you own, it is about how well you stimulate the flow of ideas. Without open and frank exchange you will fail to get the depth of insight needed.
5. Knowledge work is not about flooding people with information; it is about creating greater value for your business, its people, customers and society.

Watching our blind spots

No week can pass without us sighting an example of a business that has closed or is obviously struggling. Whether it is a government organisation like a local council or an insurance giant who has negated its obligations to its shareholders and customers, the examples are endless. The fact is businesses do not have a great track record of adapting to change.

Of course it is not just the medium to large organisations that struggle in winning the knowledge game; small business struggles as well. Just think about your local shopping, restaurant or industrial precinct, and count how many businesses have changed in the last twelve months. Each business no doubt would have a story to tell. In most cases, although they may not wish to admit it, absence of know-how or being blind to impending change may be the root cause.

A close family friend is a very successful artist who runs an art gallery. Recently, he told me this story of his attempt to build on the business but devote more time to painting. To do this he appointed a full-time gallery manager to manage the retail side of the business. In time he became concerned that given the high turnover of artwork the profitability of the business did not seem to be improving. He asked his accountant to have a closer look at the daily transactions. To his horror he discovered that over $40 000 had gone missing in a classic white-collar crime. Needless to say, when confronted the gallery manager left without a trace. Immediately my friend recruited a new gallery manager, but this time better checks and procedures—including daily reporting of transactions and regular conversations on building the potential of the business—were employed. This working relationship has more potential for success. Blind spots such as these are notoriously common in businesses.

But blind spots may not always result in a direct financial loss. The outcome could be lost or unfulfilled potential because the talent and capabilities of people are lying dormant or hidden. Organisations such as Honeywell, Microsoft, the Body Shop, Ernst & Young and Buckman Laboratories are organisations that have a track record of investing in their people by building systems that nurture and develop a winning strategy. The result is a much quicker response rate, and greater agility and adaptability to the customer.

The key to overcoming blind spots is to first recognise the danger of overconfidence and arrogance by encouraging greater honesty, disclosure and transparency. As Bill Catucci from AT&T says, 'In the past, the person reporting an unfavourable number was lonely and isolated. Now, I want people to admit to shortfalls and have everyone else respond, "How can we help?" This is an entirely new management model for the company.'

In this new model of leadership managers must support a different code of behaviour. Firstly, they must set up safe spaces in the business for people to have deep conversations on issues that they feel passionate about. This must be done without being constrained by hierarchy, ego and status. People must feel safe to be able to share their frustration, explore unresolved issues and dig for the truth. These exchanges must be undertaken in an environment of humility and humbleness. Trying to look smart is not a formula for winning the knowledge game.

Secondly, people must be prepared to coach and facilitate rather than trying to be the star. From experience, managers can be both a friend and a foe when it comes to finding smarter solutions. For example, a client of mine had a serious backlog of requests for a new home loan initiative. When I was called in to help, it became obvious very quickly that a highly motivated manager was stifling much of the initiative of the team. At the initial meeting when another member of the team raised a possible solution, the manager quickly discredited it, thereby killing off any flow of ideas. It was obvious that the current dynamics could not continue. On this occasion we took the pressure off this person to be subject-matter expert and asked them to be a coach rather than a judge. The manager played their new role beautifully and all of a sudden new natural leaders and problem solvers emerged. Within a short time the backlog problem was solved.

Finally, business must be prepared to broaden its view of the world and marketplace and be more receptive to exploring the unknown or even the unspeakable. One of my most vivid memories of a blind spot was a consulting project I undertook at the Australian Navy Supply Centre in Sydney. In the early 1990s I was asked to conduct a series of managing change training programs. At the time there was a strong rumour that the head office would soon be closed down, privatised or relocated. When I raised this scenario at the site, many of the managers and team leaders saw this scenario as totally unrealistic. They labelled it as 'consultant spook'. Their view of reality was very different. They said, why would the government touch something that is not broken. A few years later the unthinkable happened. The operation was relocated to other sites throughout Australia and many of the staff took redundancy packages. Now, where many large warehouses and offices once stood, there is a large open space being converted to an apartment complex. For me the greatest lesson in this experience was the importance of thinking outside the square.

Drawing on our courage

Make no mistake, if we want to win the knowledge game plenty of courage is needed. Why, might you say? Well, often it requires you to change or address taboos and ingrained injustice, unfairness and poor performance.

Specifically, there needs to be a strong stand to stomp out those behaviours that kill off initiative, innovation and free expression of ideas. Typically this requires us to identify and correct behaviours such as hoarding of knowledge, backstabbing and bullying—backed up with comprehensive self-improvement plans. Unfortunately, this is a tough ask when many businesses have turned such unsavoury behaviours into an art form. For example, a 2001 study by the Australian Council of Trade Unions (ACTU) found that 70 per cent of managers and supervisors had bullied their workers, and in only 18 per cent of cases was anything done about it. The ACTU also estimates that 350 000 Australians are subjected to long-term bullying, while 2.5 million people experience some type of bullying over the course of their working lives (Nixon, 2002a). A similar study by Manchester University in the UK found that over 90 per cent of respondents thought that bullies got away with their behaviour (Da Silva and L'Estrange, 2001).

It was not long ago that I presented the idea of courage at a management conference. After ending my presentation one of the participants said to me, 'Alastair, I was really interested in what you had to say about courage. In my organisation, people get beaten up for showing courage.' I responded by saying, 'Yes, you are right, but the leaders need to say we are not prepared to allow this any more. If no change occurs the epidemic will continue.'

Over the last twenty years I have seen the lack of courage and business leadership raising its ugly head time and time again. Businesses and their managers often struggle to progress because their people feel alienated, undervalued and bullied. Needless to say they are losing the knowledge game as well as business and reputation.

To redress bad behaviours there needs to be a commitment at several levels. It must start with clear evidence that the old way of managing is not only not required but is counterproductive. My experience is that if people are given the support, permission and training to act differently, they can make the necessary changes. In some of the more difficult cases, people will need a detailed performance improvement plan before real change can be observed. Even then their ego may stop them from progressing. However in most situations if the process of improvement is approached in a positive way success will result.

Most of all waiting for things to settle down rarely works. Managers need to support those people who have felt alienated or hurt by past decisions or inaction. Whatever the history, we need to take the lead and plant a new course of action. Whether it is scheduling a face-to-face meeting or going out to lunch, we must undertake a new and fresh approach to regular communication.

Letting go of control

Growing one's knowledge requires strong healthy relationships that help expand our thinking. We must listen to fresh ideas, meet different faces and find new connections. We can no longer support a world where bosses rule blindly and where people leave their brains at home.

Each day we are expected to find new answers to new situations, and this requires a better mix of thinking and collaboration.

This will often mean people talking and connecting with people who are outside their immediate work function—for example, establishing cross-functional teams or, alternatively, establishing a regular time for a wide range of people to discuss an issue of concern. For many, this may mean less emphasis on control and command, and more on encouraging new interactions across and through the business.

If you view knowledge as a prized possession that must be controlled and monitored, you will struggle in maintaining the energy and drive for innovation and business improvement. You will most likely be faced with high turnover, or worse still, a team that never contributes. Conversely, if you see knowledge as something that is in constant transition, needing to be questioned, tested and discussed, the outcome will be radically different. You will build a business culture that will be full of enterprise, promise and ideas—a business environment where people are encouraged to be helpful to each other and one free of fear and retribution.

Simple changes of leadership style can make a world of difference. However, if someone has lived their career and life hoarding knowledge and being a controlling boss, making a transition to a more inclusive approach will not be an easy one.

A person can be helped to change by providing feedback about their career, lifestyle and health. Such support and concern can often work wonders—particularly if it is backed up with concrete help and tools to make the new learning and performance improvement possible.

Championing greater sharing

The final part of building a winning strategy to knowledge and innovation is about creating an environment where sharing happens naturally. The better leaders in business use a range of tactics to help champion greater sharing. At a practical level it could include the following behaviours:

*   keeping your requests nice and simple
*   making it clear why sharing and exchange is important
*   asking of others what we would be prepared to do ourselves

- anticipating awkward situations
- starting with safe and easy changes, and then moving to more sensitive and challenging ones
- always offering to help other people in return
- thanking people for their involvement—whatever the outcome or contribution.

Developing these skills is vitally important given that, more likely than not, the person you wish to share with will have no formal reporting relationship with you. This is increasingly the case in modern business where people are working with many people in a complex web of relationships and reporting channels crossing time and place. It is not uncommon for people to have four or five people to report to in any given day. In these situations we have to work extra hard to gain commitment and trust before we can expect anything in return.

The primary goal is to encourage open sharing, irrespective of hierarchy, status or background. There must also be a clear recognition that sharing can take time and effort. So a little administrative support, and then rewarding contributors and giving social credit, can help sway the balance in your favour.

In saying this we do need to see the difference between just chatting aimlessly and exploring what matters. Often people say to me, we do knowledge sharing as we have meetings. From years of observation, many such gatherings only go through the motions. They are full of tightly controlled agendas, undiscussed assumptions and never-to-be-revealed viewpoints. The fact is when you experience knowledge sharing at its best you can certainly feel the difference because it is full of excellent dialogue, commitment and a desire to take responsibility.

Again we need to champion the cause of winning the knowledge game by first being prepared to open hearts and minds. If our personal behaviour is at odds with what we expect of others, we can hardly expect others to assist. See it as your personal goal to be a role model of greater collaboration, networking and celebration of knowing. Coach people to take responsibility for what they are passionate about, and encourage people to discover and learn together. Be generous with your knowledge.

Summary

To be truly successful in putting knowledge to work we need to have a clear focus, engage motivation and build the right systems. We need to be aware of biases, our blind spots and beliefs, and be courageous enough to discover what we do not know. We must be prepared to let go of control and command and sponsor two-way flow between a wide range of people. Taking an expansive attitude can change our lives and help us win through better know-how and insight.

CHAPTER 2

Building trust and support

'When the spirit of people is strong, focused and vibrant, wonderful things begin to happen.'
—HARRISON OWEN

Building trust and support requires:

- greater respect and appreciation
- different networks, connections and friendships
- procedural fairness and transparency
- awareness of our respective trust levels
- seeing relapses as a natural part of personal growth.

Sponsoring greater partnering

Building knowledge requires trust. Whether it is employees making new plans, or a consortium of companies teaming together for a new venture, there must be a degree of cohesion and openness before the desired rewards can be expected. Without trust, the potential for innovation and discovery becomes very limited. All the words and intentions in the world will not make a scrap of difference if it is not backed up with a genuine desire to share ideas, feelings and plans.

The list of trust-building behaviours can appear quite overwhelming at times, and so it is important to keep them as simple as possible. Recognise that the journey is not an easy one and that there will be moments of contradiction and ambiguity along the way. Be prepared to dust off some bad habits and give it a try.

To help you build the potential for opening hearts and minds to knowledge-sharing experiences, here are five cornerstones of trust that can assist in the process:

1. Where possible, seek out opportunities for higher levels of trust by raising issues of concern along the way, while avoiding premature judgments based on incorrect assumptions or conclusions. Be prepared to forgive, show concern and demonstrate compassion.
2. Take the time to establish the ground rules on how knowledge sharing might work in practice. Simply asking what the other party desires and expects in an exchange can make a world of difference.
3. Trust is built on competence; be a manager who is prepared to build and foster openness, transparency and frank exchange. Ensure promises are backed up with mutually agreed actions. Take the time and effort to jointly celebrate discoveries, insights and adventures. Always avoid behaviours that reduce trust, such as talking behind people's backs or failing to deliver as agreed.
4. If you are not happy in a relationship or exchange be prepared to say so. Wasting time and energy when you are not happy will not serve anyone's interest. Clarify what can be delivered. Do not get angry; just get clear.
5. When the exchange is not working, ask for feedback on what you can do to stimulate the relationship. If you find that you cannot meet expectations or it is simply not the right time, say thanks, and

move on. Do not lay blame; just move on. There are many other people you could be relating to—so get on with it.

Making solid progress in trust often requires us to clear emotional baggage that may be limiting us from operating in a greater zone of intimacy. We must be prepared to clear beliefs, uncertainties and the pain that may be holding us back from fully trusting or being open. If we want to build new high-trust relationships it is quite likely we will need to revisit a long list of memories—some painful and some joyful. Typically, these ghosts from the past could be those involving us being let down and being hurt, while the joyful memories could include wonderful moments of high team spirit, exchange and innovation. To build trust we need to recognise that clearing our past is a major factor in being able to move forward.

The reality is that people are naturally cautious; they need proof that disclosure is safe and that anything you learn will not be used inappropriately. For trust to exist there must be high levels of rapport and reciprocal exchange, and in most situations that does not exist. We are therefore left with the unfortunate reality that we have to do the best we can with the trust we have been given. Then assuming you are able to spark a positive exchange, what will a person choose to share? Will they do enough to just get rid of you? Or will they actively want to help you? Even then, is the information you receive relevant and will you act on it? Or will the knowledge you receive be filtered to such an extent that it is worthless? Alternatively, they may just not know or be unable to share what they know. Often the pearls of wisdom we need are locked way in the mind and nobody can access them. Such questions are integral to the skill of building trust and can only be resolved by having close and intimate conversations with people over time.

Of course having long and intimate conversations is becoming more difficult in a world dominated by email, telephone and text messages. Somehow we need to step out of the 'busyness' of modern living and make sure we rekindle deeper relationships with key people—whether it is over lunch or contacting someone once a month for a longer and more informal chat. For trust to blossom, be prepared to build a spirit of belonging that goes further than just the job or the area of discussion. Taking the extra trouble to express your wishes and intentions will dramatically improve the capacity for a high trust relationship to be maintained. In some cases people may not want to partner with you and that is acceptable; we need to see that as understandable. Instead of becoming frustrated by people who do not wish to partner, we should react by seeing this as perfectly normal. There needs to be a deeper understanding of what is allowable and permissible. Key in long-term business relationships is shared advantage and partnering.

Reviewing our inner circle

We need only ask people how they acquire knowledge to quickly understand how often they rely on a few trusted friends. For example, if you decide to buy a new home entertainment system do you unconditionally accept what you first see, read or hear, or do you ask a few trusted people for their opinions? We are all likely to place much more value on what a trusted friend or adviser says rather than relying totally on the advice of someone unknown.

This trait of the web of human connection has profound implications on our ability to grow and learn. If our network of contacts is too small or narrow, we will not have the pool of collective wisdom we need to manage the myriad challenges that lie ahead. It is quite likely that in 90 per cent of cases we will need to go well outside our circle of close friends and advisers. However, in reality, due to the personal weighting we tend to give to our connections, we do the opposite, staying with those trusted few to help us solve nearly everything we face.

Of course, changing or expanding our mix of close contacts is not always easy, particularly given the pressures of time. But we do need to think more creatively about how we can adapt our personal networks and business connections. Unless we make this effort we most likely will be operating in a vacuum.

Having done much of the hard work on improving levels of trust we then need to become skilled in deciding who should be part of our more trusted circle of advisers, mentors or helpers. As mentioned, we commonly rely on a very small group of individuals to be our most trusted inner circle. Typically, a manager would have up to 150 individuals to whom he or she turns for advice or information. However, their inner circle can be much smaller. This network of high-trust relationships can include many people from work colleagues, associates, acquaintances or relatives. It is here that the most intimate knowledge is often shared.

This inner circle of trusted friends is built up over time and we are often quite resistant to changing its composition. Why, might you say? Well, we feel connected emotionally and it is here where we feel most comfortable. In most cases people are very protective of their inner circle, whether it is just habit or it just feels nice and cosy. For example, reflect on a recent experience where someone has demanded or requested more time from you. This could be someone who wants to spend more time with you socially. Do you automatically say yes, or do you consider the cost of spending more time with that person and less with someone else?

Like many others, changing my inner circle has been and continues to be a huge issue. For example, each year I get countless requests from other prospective or actual authors who want to write with me. This is in addition to the many external consultants and contractors who want to be part of my business. Each time I receive these requests, I have to make a decision that evaluates the potential benefit of joint writing or partnering. The decisions are rarely easy, but there are times when I have to stretch my comfort zone and change my inner circle based on different circumstances.

Reviewing and changing our inner circle is particularly important given the changing nature of work and life. Where the issues we are now facing are in constant flux, so should be our network of contacts. How we vary and change our personal networks can have a profound impact on our capacity to cope and self-manage. Certainly advances such as the Internet and devices such as mobile telephones have improved our opportunities for mixing with a more diverse group of people. However, often the level of intimacy can suffer, particularly when face-to-face conversations are lacking.

Ultimately, however, being stuck in a zone of similar-thinking people can help with some challenges but could be quite dangerous for others. This is commonly seen in business, when decision makers are unable to respond correctly to what is happening. Be prepared to review your connections on a regular basis. This may not be as radical as crossing names out of a personal organiser or diary, but it does mean becoming more aware of the strengths and weaknesses of your existing network of knowledge, and being prepared to make the required changes. This is certainly not one of the easier parts of winning the knowledge game, but it is probably one of the more important.

Securing exchange on a free and fair basis

Developing a spirit of reciprocity and fairness is a very misunderstood area of trust development. Just because an employer hires someone does not mean they will openly discuss their ideas and freely give their full attention and commitment. People need to feel that the exchange is fair and free. In other words they must feel that what eventuates will not bleed them dry and leave them feeling vulnerable or unwanted. Deciding not to share is often an indicator that a person does not feel quite right in the existing arrangement, resulting in them not sharing being a much safer option. In many cases, reassurance, education and coaching needs to be backed up with a guarantee of fair treatment so that efforts will be recognised and protected. The benefits of sharing must be greater than the costs.

In business, free and fair treatment is equally important for all forms of employment whether full time, part time or contract. It is also just as important for that one-off request, or pleas for help. Let us say a manager is seeking answers or help from someone whom they have never met, or someone whom they have met once and are unlikely to ever meet again. The manager must guarantee that what is learnt will be used fairly and the source will be recognised. That means securing agreement on how the knowledge will be used and how each party will benefit. This is recommended even when the issue of fairness or freedom to act is not raised. It is better to be safe, and this means not taking things for granted.

This is particularly the case when it comes to more sensitive matters such as protecting intellectual property and trade secrets. Even if other people do not ask for such guarantees, you need to ensure the appropriate level of respect, appreciation and support is observed. In practice, this means creating trust-forming relationships where both parties feel, hear and see the benefit in the exchange—thereby ensuring that what is shared or given will be somehow acknowledged in full. Then if permission is given, the original contributor is acknowledged. This practice, where original idea creators are credited for their thinking, not only builds a public standing of excellence, but also provides a powerful message that wisdom and insight are fully appreciated and valued.

Securing a fair process means creating procedures that reward the sharing of knowledge. Tangibly this would mean rewarding people who sponsor free exchange of knowledge, such as coaches, innovators and mentors. This may mean some monetary remuneration but more often than not it has nothing to do with salary. People want to see that ideas are used with integrity and credit.

Other strategies regularly used in business include rewarding the best sharers and coaches by being part of privileged gatherings such as think-tanks at residential venues, study groups or including them in future succession plans. Needless to say, people who intentionally steal other people's ideas are scorned at. What is encouraged is building a network of people who praise and celebrate inventiveness, creativity and application.

Working at our highest level of trust

To build rapport and openness it is important to work at our highest level of trust. Stuart Wells (1997) discusses four levels of trust, which provide a useful framework for building the relationships you need to win the knowledge game. The premise behind this framework is that you can evolve to a higher level of trust at any time if both parties are prepared to partner at the level. The four levels are:

1. The lowest level of trust is *negotiated trust*. Here both parties only act on those matters which have been clearly agreed to. Detailed actions and milestones would be a central part of this agreement. This is often seen in early discussions between untrusting parties.
2. The next level of trust is *conditional trust*. In this context people work on the assumption that the other party will get the benefit of your doubt until you see how they perform. If they do well, or they meet your expectations, you will trust them more. Here you are setting up an often unspecified probation period for the other party to prove their worth and trustworthiness. This is a little more liberating and freewheeling than the negotiated level of trust.
3. The third level of trust is *cooperative trust*, which works on the belief that if a party fails to meet its commitments it does not automatically

mean that trust will be eroded. You realise that all parties will sometimes experience difficulties and these will be sorted out. What is more important is building a long-term relationship.

4. *Unconditional trust* is the highest level of trust. This relies on the deepest integrity and intention of all. Here you are not concerned about the levels of trust; you have moved onto more enlightened perspectives, such as bringing about required change, making positive reform and sponsoring innovation. As a result, you begin spending your energies on getting on with the job rather than checking and balancing the behaviour or performance of the other party. If a situation arises that is not desired, there is faith that the problem will be discussed and resolved.

In applying this model, one soon discovers that many deeper questions or issues about trust bubble to the surface. For example, in recent times I have pondered the following questions:

- What level of trust am I capable of, when giving or receiving?
- What can be done to improve the level of trust and/or trust-worthiness?
- What are the advantages and disadvantages of trusting more?
- What are the possible consequences of my current level of trust?
- Do the costs of trusting more outweigh the benefits?
- Am I displaying the right level of checks and balances?

Responding to relapses

As already emphasised, the right level of trust is imperative if we wish to win the knowledge game. However, in saying this, we also need to accept that relapses are a fact of life, whether it is changing our diet, giving up smoking or building trust. Why, might you say? Well, like any habit, it often takes many attempts before we can perfect the new skill. So instead of seeing relapses as a problem, we should see them as a perfectly normal part of the personal growth process.

So if you wish to help build trust, spend your time and energy in rewarding the desired behaviour and remind people how their world will change if they are successful in cementing a different habit. From experience, it is far better for a manager to give praise and build confidence than lay blame. We need to remind people of why the effort is necessary and encourage them to continue. This also goes for us changing our habits. We need to be kind to ourselves when we experience relapses, and get ready to steer ourselves back on course. Where possible we need to learn the lesson of why a relapse might have occurred, stop being angry or frustrated, remind ourselves of our goal and get back on track. Then make a special effort to acknowledge our feelings and make sure we give ourselves the time and space to take corrective action.

We also need to understand that building trust can create a tension of win–lose. This is particularly so if people feel they are losing power from changing the nature of their personal relationships and how knowledge is shared. This vulnerability is common, particularly if a person is used to being an independent contributor or feels that the status of someone is above or below them. Most of all, we need to let people know that they are accepted for who they are, and that you want them to be part of a new way of relating. That way, you have a much better chance of building a shared purpose that will stimulate greater levels of commitment and responsibility. The wonderful thing is that when trust exists the process of knowledge and innovation is so much easier.

One technique, which demonstrates many of the qualities of high trust, is 'Open Space'. Open Space is a group technique practised by Harrison Owen (2000), a North American consultant. The Open Space technique draws on the wisdom of indigenous groups, notably in the village of Balamah in Western Africa, the Native American tradition and the Far East. Harrison Owen shows how a simple group process can be used to help build trust, shared purpose and higher levels of awareness.

The Open Space process asks people to address concerns and actions on a specific issue. To be successful the people involved must feel passionate and care about the issue being discussed. For example, reducing wastage, ideas for a new marketing campaign or fund-raising for a school fete could be topics in the right context. The thinking behind Open Space is that people can quickly and instantaneously create solutions without massive amounts of preparation and external assistance. In this process people are allowed over a period of one to three days to work through issues without the imposition of fixed agendas and tightly controlled presentations. Typically, people stand or sit in a circle and engage in dialogue, which leads to a higher level of understanding and clarity. In doing so, they normally follow a number of simple ground rules. These include:

- giving maximum opportunity for each person to contribute
- if a person feels that they are not learning or contributing they can leave
- all issues raised will be discussed unless it is decided not to do so
- no prescribed outcome is allowed to dictate the process.

At the end of the meeting, the proceedings are produced in a hard-copy format or published on an easily edited e-version on the Internet or intranet site or business portal. This commitment to action often leads to the establishment of action groups and areas of activity, which leads to breakthroughs in knowledge, insight and action.

In recent years, more sophisticated advances in technology are being used to encourage further collaboration and teaming via advances such as virtual chat rooms, file sharing, videoconferencing, webcam and search engine capabilities. However, the traditional enablers such as face-to-face conversations, email, telephone and facsimile are still the most common modes of communication.

Interestingly, the most value occurs with Open Space when things are not easy to resolve; the method is of most value when there is no simple solution, and there is a high potential for creative tension and exchange. It is in this domain that landmark discoveries and innovation are more likely to occur.

Summary

Trust is the life force of knowledge. The higher the trust the greater the potential for the sharing of knowledge. To become better in building trust there needs to be a clear acceptance that trust may be limited, is hard earned and can be easily lost. In many ways, it does not happen naturally for people. Building trust requires a faith that people with the right level of responsibility and fairness can help others to successfully learn and work together. In time, our capacity to build trust will depend not only on how trust is received, but how we view trust ourselves. One method that helps build high levels of trust is Open Space.

CHAPTER 3

Expanding your thinking

'Present-thinking people kill the future.'
—KEN BLANCHARD

Expanding our thinking requires:

- knowing the special abilities that drive our expertise
- exploring big, hairy and audacious goals
- discovering what we do not know
- sharing the benefits of what we do know
- healthy questioning of our plans and actions.

Being ready for tomorrow

In the modern business world, everything can be rosy and then with a blink of an eye our whole future can become very, very cloudy. It was only a few years ago that Bill Gates said Microsoft needed to change every two years or it would go out of business. Now the life cycle in the software industry is much shorter. It is now not unusual for businesses in this industry to talk about three-month planning scenarios.

Book and music shops are another example of just how quickly things can change. Many are finding they must have an Internet presence to compete with the 'amazon.coms' of this world. Such queue jumping in the supply chain has become very common with access to instant information via the Internet being so prevalent. Such a profound change has created a whole new marketplace dominated by e-commerce, branding and cyberspace, rather than by where customers live and work.

Certainly with modern change, there is a whole new pressure on our ability to grow our know-how. Being a market leader is increasingly meaningless if customers can discover and find better options elsewhere. A year can now feel like a lifetime. It was recently expressed to me that we are now living in dog years—that is, for each of our human years it now feels like we are living seven. Everything seems to be happening at a million kilometres an hour. Such a pace of change can make us feel out of control. However, it is not all bad news. Living with change can also be incredibly exciting and invigorating, particularly if we are motivated enough to learn smarter and pool expertise to meet the challenges that lie ahead.

In a dynamic world dominated by economic, social and political change, we cannot wait for the luxury of things to settle down. We must use our know-how to anticipate and respond to the specific changes affecting our own world. In business, this means being ready to anticipate what may happen next. This may involve exploring the changing needs of your customers, varying market conditions, or any other factor that may threaten the future success of your business.

Dorothy Leonard (1998), the author of *Wellsprings of Knowledge*, discusses how our capabilities and expertise can be both helpful and a hindrance. Our knowledge can quickly become a problem if it fails to adapt to changes and challenges. A business rigidity like a capability can be in the form of a skill, managerial system or a belief, but what gets a business or career into trouble is when our expertise and know-how is at odds with where we need to go next. For example, Polaroid, the once proud international business, ceased trading in 2001. The business could not change its core expertise from negative film processing to the world of digital imaging. Polaroid's core capability had reached its use-by date. As Dorothy Leonard also explains, NASA is another prime example of how capabilities must change. The capabilities and expertise that helped NASA land a man on the moon in 1969 are not the same as those needed to land a human on Mars.

The lessons of Polaroid and NASA are transferable to every business in society, whether it is growing crops on a farm, changing the menu in a food bar or revamping the curriculum at a university. Our desire to modify our thinking and advance our capabilities is essential. However, what makes this discussion on capabilities so important is that the habits of an individual and the capabilities of a business are not easily changed. Even with clear evidence for change, people must be motivated to make the change and to reposition their knowledge.

One of the joys and burdens of winning the knowledge game is that our talents and abilities often lie deeply hidden in our minds. It is easy to think that the success of a business is its brand, its location or an innovative design, but what is important is how these qualities or capabilities are nurtured and sustained. For example, 3M's success is based on both its understanding of abrasives and an organisational culture where leaders actively encourage ideas from anywhere at any time. Such business self-awareness is priceless.

Dorothy Leonard suggests that one practical way to map our business capabilities is to examine your last five innovations. Where did you draw your knowledge from and what form did it take? Was it a physical asset, specific expertise or an attitude driving your success? Asking and answering questions such as these will help you to identify and learn from your business experience and be more successful in uncovering deeper knowledge and insight.

It is amazing how many managers are insulated from an honest assessment of their capabilities, whether it is in the private or government sector, in large or small business. Often decisions are made with insufficient knowledge and scanning of the environment and they are unaware of strengths and weaknesses. The result is a series of biased, subjective and filtered conclusions, and very poor action. As will be discussed in

Chapter 6 on 'Creating a smarter business', many decision makers are decades behind in how they screen and scan their competitive environment. This is particularly the case for smaller and medium-sized businesses, where such analysis and thinking is often seen as too expensive, time-consuming and complex. However, this need not be the case.

Competitive intelligence and deeper thinking about our capabilities with the right level of planning and implementation can pay for itself with better results and business advantage. Although market signals are rarely easy to read, asking the right questions can make a big difference, particularly if more effort is spent gaining quality data and insight from the right people. Needless to say relying on a few trusted friends, or just reading a one-page news summary, is hardly sufficient in today's marketplace. We need to be much more clever and sophisticated in order to be successful. Finding out too late is a luxury no one can afford. We need to build a business attitude where everyone keeps their eyes and ears open to important signals in the marketplace to ensure our capabilities are relevant.

To do this requires us to stretch our imagination from the likely and predictable to the unthinkable or non-predictable. In a practical sense, drafting a plan for learning and action is a great start. To do this, you should be asking yourself which capabilities you want to have in twelve months' time. Then list and complete the actions that will help you get there. Such planning can be a wonderful safeguard in an ever-changing world.

We need only ponder for a minute some of changes that have affected our lives during the last few years. Few CEOs would have predicted the World Trade Center attack in New York on 11 September 2001. Lloyd's of London estimated that as much as US$10 billion was lost from business interruption alone—that is, corporate losses caused directly by the severing of networks housing critical customer and financial data and the resultant transportation gridlock. This loss was greater in many businesses because of a lack of secondary back-up systems. Interestingly, there was at least one exception: General Electric had a contingency back-up plan just in case such an event did occur. Within thirty minutes of the attack, the systems and data that were lost in the attack were backed up and replaced from alternative sources. All this thinking was done in General Electric's scenario and contingency planning well in advance.

So the message of adaptability, agility and flexibility is central to winning the knowledge game. Take another issue like public health. Public-health employees are under constant pressure to meet the expectations of patients/clients, the media, voters, politicians and legislation, often with very limited resources and budgets. Then depending on the issue of the day, the priorities can change overnight and staff must be ready to adapt and respond with hardly a moment's notice.

Breaking our limits

One of the most common mistakes we make is that we become stuck with only one view of the future. Whether a sports coach, a small business operator or planning for a weekend holiday, predicting what may or may not happen next is part of life. The skill of opening our minds to the future is vitally important if we wish to organise our resources and capabilities to meet the next challenge.

As already explained, our level of preparedness is a major factor in how well we will cope. We need to encourage people to open their thinking to new thoughts and perceptions. As Gary Haseldine from Haseldine Winners International says, 'success is only a new thought away'. However, if we paralyse ourselves with unnecessary limits, our capacity to evolve and adapt will be limited. Expanding our thinking requires us to question our self-imposed labels, values and attitudes. Winning the knowledge game is a process of growth based on critical review and examination. Business can only change direction or people can only change their lives by altering and adjusting their attitudes.

The best way of expanding our thinking is to allow the unthinkable or uncomfortable to be said. A low tolerance for different or eccentric thinking is a recipe for business demise and stagnation. Similarly, we cannot expect people to be thrown into a meeting room and be creative, leading edge and groundbreaking. We need to create the environment and a system to help toss ideas around. We need to ensure that people have the right energy and inspiration to expand their levels of thinking. Brian Garrett, CEO of the Commonwealth Scientific and Industrial Research Organisation (CSIRO), requested when he first arrived in the business in 2000, 'big hairy and audacious goals for the future'. In doing so he helped shape a new direction.

Understandably, people are uncomfortable thinking away from the present. Ann Andrews, from a business called Teams From Woe To Go, recently shared the remarkable results from a survey of Fortune 500 companies. In the study, leaders were asked what percentage of their time they spent planning for their future. What would be your answer? Maybe 50 per cent, 20 per cent, 10 per cent or even less? Well the answer was 3 per cent. Needless to say if you feel uncomfortable about future planning you are not alone; it is perfectly normal to feel anxious and a little nervous about the process. However, modern business managers must do much more thinking about their future. It is my experience that most career, life and business planning is at best scratchy, shallow and conservative. Typically, the limited thinking manifests itself as simple predictions based on known events, which leads to very few surprises and it rarely prepares people for what is going to happen next. People may have been able to rely on such thinking a hundred years ago, but it is certainly fraught with danger in the chaotic world of the twenty-first century.

To help people sharpen their thinking about their limits and possibilities, teams need to be established to help people study the future. I have found that encouraging people to reframe their thinking can be a major asset to building expanded imagination and insight. For example, asking 'what if' questions can be very worthwhile—that is, taking the time to frame questions using the words 'what if' as an opener. Recent questions I have asked with a banking client included:

- What if interest rates dropped by 0.5 per cent?
- What if funding were slashed by 15 per cent?
- What if you do not get the new staff member by July?

In a similar vein IBM, like many other businesses, has learned to use 'so what' questions to grow their business capacity. For example, let us assume a competitor is launching a new product or service. The response might be, 'so what'. This 'so what' question could create a new insight that might better prepare the business for the future.

Inspiring a worthwhile purpose

Gone are the days when people could go about their business with scant disregard for the ramifications of their actions on others. We are increasingly expected to be a corporate citizen who demonstrates a clear social charter and responsibility to society, rather than just being preoccupied with profit and shareholder return.

Aiming a little higher and broader can make a world of difference to the support you will receive for your business, and provide greater potential for long-term success. As Dr Ronald Forbes, from the Leaderskill Group in Sydney, reminded me in a timely email: 'if the benefit of what you and your business do does not add to the well-being of the planet, society or the client, you should scrap it'. He went on to say, 'if you take this stand you will find that people will respect you more and you will feel a greater buzz in what you are doing. Such intention will enable you to see the gaps in your current approach and will lead to higher levels of accountability, transparency and integrity.'

Here are some examples of how different thinking and/or a sharper focus can affect business strategy and process:

- Kodak moved from the photography business to the memory business.
- Scandinavian Airlines moved from flying planes to flying people.
- A counselling service moved from offering marriage counselling to relationship counselling.
- A health-care provider moved from providing health-care administration on breast cancer to a focus on saving lives.
- A theatre company became an entertainment business for the local community.

Of course to arrive at such resolutions, we need to understand our market and business environment. There must be an honest assessment of capabilities based on current and future trends. Such an assessment will usually lead to a number of trends being explored, including:

- technological
- demographic/societal
- business culture
- leadership
- economic and financial
- global
- environmental
- organisational capacity

- individual cap;.city and morale
- customer expectations
- political/government pressures
- regional or local issues.

An analysis of trends such as these will help you and your business become more acutely aware of strengths and weaknesses, while also becoming clearer about the specific knowledge and capabilities that need nurturing.

Of course the benefits of these conversations will not occur overnight. Deeper and far-reaching explorations need to be part of the corporate or business psyche. In some cases it could take three to six months before any workable and agreed strategies can be attained. This will particularly be the case if this type of thinking is seen as unusual and unnatural. In a more stable business environment such scenario thinking should be seriously considered every two years. How far you look ahead will depend on the nature of the business. For example, Honeywell in 1998 set up a global think-tank process over several months looking at the year 2010; CSIRO looked twenty-five years ahead in 2001; and the country of Singapore has done similarly in their mission to become an 'Intelligent Island'.

Bringing in new points of view

One of the practical realities of expanding our thinking is that we listen to new and different points of view. Whether it is having a conversation with an industry authority, reading more widely, and/or attending a trade conference, it is imperative that we are open to different messages.

In practice, this could mean bringing together thought leaders or experts into a business process, organising a monthly breakfast among some industry observers or planting a devil's advocate into a debate. It could also involve holding research interviews with customers, clients or colleagues before proceeding with action. Such a mobilisation of wisdom is vital in today's business world.

During the last fifteen years, I have been lucky to be part of many groundbreaking business processes that have stretched people's imagination. For example, at Coca-Cola, during a strategic planning launch, we invited a major customer to share what they liked and disliked about the current service. This input helped put the whole change process into context. With other businesses, I have asked teams to undertake field research before attending a planning meeting. Such preparation can make a world of difference to the end result.

Goran Carstedt, a past senior manager in IKEA Europe, tells the story of how he would often hover around the car parks outside his retail outlets to discover customer reactions and needs. In other businesses, key people are sent into different marketplaces, countries and regions to discover how they can deliver better service. I know from personal experience that the better senior executives make it their business to find the time to listen to their front-line staff, customers, suppliers and other stakeholders.

So what do you do if this premise of bringing in new points of view and expanding your thinking is a whole new skill? Why not follow this simple method suggested by Brandan Hall, a leading authority on e-learning in the US. He suggests the following five-step process:

1. Photocopy a yearly calendar for the next five years.
2. Spend three solid hours with pen and paper in a 'soulful place', and speculate about the future.
3. Interview five 'internal customers' about their views.
4. Interview five vendors, suppliers or customers.
5. Set up a think-tank (e.g. working breakfasts/lunches) with others to create alternative scenarios for the future.

Implementing smarter actions

Coming up with great ideas is one thing, but we also need a good action plan. Expanding our thinking must continue into implementation. Often managers make the mistake of leaving their creativity behind when it comes to key milestones, actions and responsibilities. Done well, action planning and review is where most of our critical business learning will occur.

For me, giving myself the permission to undertake different approaches to planning has dramatically improved my expertise, confidence and success in achieving goals, while also learning more. It also helped remove much of the pain, struggle and anguish from the more stretching goals.

One approach to action planning and review is called 'Backwards Planning'. For example, let us assume you wanted to create an Internet home page. There is a series of incremental steps that need to be followed to achieve this goal. Starting at an end point of a completed home page, you would list actions and outcomes in reverse order from completion to the start. Let us say over a thirty-day period you make comments every five days (e.g. Day 25, Day 20, Day 15 and so on). You would then list observable actions at each of these days. Of course the time frames will vary depending on the project, but the idea of Backwards Planning will remain. For example, when I was completing the second draft for this book, I gave myself eight days between 23 December and 7 January. I then mapped out a measurable plan to achieve my goal, while also finding time for other parts of my life over the Christmas and New Year period.

As well as developing a carefully crafted plan, it is also helpful to have checks and balances to ensure that we do not fall into the trap of jumping into quick-fix solutions. Instead of racing into premature action without thinking, we may need to stop and ponder. Questions that can help to expand our thinking include:

- How would you describe what you are trying to solve or fix?
- What are the consequences of the current situation?
- What is your desired outcome?
- What is your normal or quick-fix solution to this situation?
- What could be the negative and positive consequences of taking this action?
- Given these observations, how would you redefine your solution or strategy?

However, most of all we need to be ready with an action plan that has anticipated our likely risks and threats and opportunities. Such planning is vital where a loss or gain of reputation and/or a disruption to business can have enormous consequences. Begin with listing the consequences and responses to fluctuations to staffing, networks, communications and systems. Then test your draft plan with so-called pre-scripted scenarios, and then see how your draft plan stacks up. From there you can review and build your capability with a sensible plan, backed up with the right level of funding, know-how and measurement.

Summary

Expansive thinking is a mandatory part of putting knowledge to work. We must be open to exploring new methods for planning and preparing ourselves for action and learning. Staying comfortable within our known universe is a recipe for disaster. We must be prepared to go to new places and find new answers. Whether it is becoming more curious in what we do, or asking clients and customers for their opinions, we must be better prepared for surprises and the unthinkable, and be prepared to dig out and uncover those special abilities we will need for the future.

CHAPTER 4

Faster, deeper learning

'Busy people must find even more time for reflection and checking in.'—Lyn Bousefield

Faster, deeper learning requires:

- trusting our intuition
- reviewing what we have learnt
- archiving our stories, facts and wisdom
- using advances in digital technology
- building a network of generous sharers.

Learning in a 15-minute world

The story of Carol and Victor

It is 4.45 pm on a typical working day for Carol and Victor. They are in their small home office in the inner city. At the front door is a courier tapping her foot, expecting immediate attention. Both Carol and Victor are preoccupied.

In the next 15 minutes Carol needs to finish an Internet search on Indonesia's current economic situation. She needs to contribute to a telephone conference call on export opportunities in Indonesia at 5 pm with her major client. Victor is also frantically trying to get on top of his workload. He is already two days behind in his emails and the taxation department is chasing the latest financials. On top of this he is struggling to prepare for an upcoming exam at university. He is seriously thinking of dropping out and enrolling in an e-learning program instead.

Needless to say Carol and Victor are feeling swamped. The courier has her demands too—she is expected to complete four more deliveries before 5.30 pm. She wants to make the fast train home, so that she can keep her commitment to coach the local girl's basketball team at 7 pm.

The story of Carol and Victor is indicative of what most of us face on a daily basis. We are living in a '15-minute world', where people struggle not only to do their job well and meet their obligations, but also to do the learning and activities they desire to keep up to date and fulfilled.

In the 15-minute world, we are expected to respond to and meet every obligation. It can at times be uncompromising. If left unchecked, we can quickly become burnt out and unproductive. Apart from escaping to a retreat somewhere in the country, or locking the doors to our home, or turning off all digital and electrical appliances, we all have to face the 15-minute world on a daily basis. We can easily become so busy that we never discover better ways of doing things. As a result, we can quickly fall into the trap of living a life full of 'busyMess' and not 'busyness'. This is a central challenge in modern business and has profound implications for how we win the knowledge game. Managers and businesses must find better ways of stepping outside this frantic 15-minute world, and discover what is vital and important. At first such an investment may seem odd and out of character, but unless managers think deeply about their critical challenges they will never obtain the insight they need to move their businesses and lives forward with more imagination and potential.

Of course the 15-minute world may not be all that bad; there is a certain excitement and engagement that comes from a busy fast-paced life. However, if our desire is to also live a smarter and more enjoyable existence, we must really think about how to avoid some of the potential traps of the 15-minute world. Such traps include trying to do too much, being too busy to really notice what is going on, failing to prioritise and not reducing or eliminating unnecessary costs and activity.

Similarly, by not letting the 15-minute world dominate us, we increase our chances of being more reflective and aware of people's concerns and expectations. This means a greater potential for empathy, compassion and a real understanding of what is actually going on. It helps us to trust our intuition. On a personal level, I have found regular meditation helps me to clear my mind and take a fresh look at situations. By taking a few moments each day to notice my breathing and state of mind, I can not only build a clearer view of what is really happening, but I also create a mind space where new insight can bubble to the surface. During the four years I have been practising meditation, I have found I have more creativity and energy to fight the harder challenges in life by staying a little calmer. Whatever method you use, whether it is taking time to sit in a park or undertaking a little exercise, do something each day to check into your mind on a regular basis. Such discipline will certainly help you to respond to the complexities, demands and pressures of modern living.

Going beyond speed

Many of us have heard the story of the tortoise and the hare, where the tortoise calmly walks during the race, eventually beating the much faster and frantic rival. A similar story is told in Japanese culture where two Samurai warriors are racing through a field of long bamboo. The Samurai who takes the time to stop and sharpen his sword is victorious.

Such simple wisdom—that we need to reflect and catch our breath—is vitally important when it comes to putting knowledge to work. Speed, and being fast by itself, is not enough.

I remember presenting my first training session in Singapore, where I was using a combination of PowerPoint slides and small group activities. I had been told that in Singapore it was customary to present very quickly, with many visuals and minimal interaction. Learners wanted to collect the information quickly and leave with the collected ideas for future use. At the time this raised a tremendous dilemma for me, because over the past twenty years I had learnt that the best learning occurs when people stop racing and opportunities are created for interaction, the sharing of insight and collaboration.

As I adapted my training style to the Singaporean culture, I quickly discovered that my assumptions were also correct in their culture. All I needed to do was to spend a little more time gaining permission for involvement and making sure people felt safe before expecting them to express their views and be actively involved. My newly adapted style led to greater learning and flow because the training delivery was correctly paced, and people were able to share key issues and discoveries as they occurred. Since then, this insight of gaining permission has helped me to adapt my training style to other cultures as well.

The lesson behind this training scenario translates into other business situations. It could be a team meeting, a chat over a business lunch or having a conversation on the Internet—all need the right level of permission, interaction and openness for faster and deeper learning to occur.

Clearly, moving from a world of speed to one of combining speed with depth will for many people be an unnatural act. It requires breaking lifetime habits and developing new skills of reflection and review. It also requires mutual support and peer assistance that is often sadly lacking. For example, if a manager is working in a business that is in constant crisis and chaos, it makes our task of learning somewhat harder. However, there are some simple things you can do to help.

Firstly, organise the right time and place for deeper conversations. Certainly, there are times when you will need to farm out high volumes of information, but there are also times when you should slow down and encourage deeper reflection. One such example was recently shared by Cris Townley from Deloitte Touche Tohmatsu, in a Standards Australia National Conference on Knowledge Management. Cris discussed how carefully organised and facilitated lunches between business partners have helped create a much-needed cross-fertilisation of ideas. She uses the metaphor of seeing the lunch gatherings as bringing the various nomadic campfires together to build higher levels of support and know-how in the business.

Secondly, be prepared to move beyond just doing activities and tasks, and encourage people to learn from what they are doing. This is particularly tough in a project-driven business, where the next task is always the next thing on the agenda. So somewhere, we must create different dynamics for people to better circulate and apply their know-how. According to Ron Sanchez (2001), a European authority on organisational learning, there are a number of processes that knowledge must travel through in a business for there to be healthy learning.

First of all, individuals must create knowledge. This knowledge is then shared within groups. The groups then use their knowledge to understand coordinated action and to jointly develop new capabilities. Finally, groups share their knowledge with other groups to generate a business-wide benefit. This flow and transfer of knowledge is the heartbeat of business change and innovation. For an organisational learning cycle to be successful, knowledge must be explored and evaluated by a combination of individuals and groups who passionately believe in the benefit of building and sharing wisdom.

Sanchez also explains that for healthy business learning to occur, there must be an understanding that learning fundamentally occurs in the minds of individuals as they try to make sense of their world. For example, what we believe to be true (or in other words, what we think we know) must always be subject to ongoing testing and validation. We must be willing to replace old beliefs, old knowledge and models. An individual manager, like anyone else in a business, must convincingly explain their ideas to others before those ideas will ever become accepted or be seen as credible. The essential role of managers must be done in a spirit of exploration, support and stimulation for it to generate breakthrough thinking and innovation. When we interact and collaborate with others in seeking to raise the level of wisdom, we need to tune into three basic problems:

1. People may know more than they say.
2. People may say more than they know.

3. People place their own meanings on what they hear, see or experience.

There are many ways of generating a spirit of exchange and of ensuring learning is both deeper and faster. In later chapters, several ways of doing this will be explained; for the moment, here are three practical suggestions for stimulating deeper and faster learning: Learning Journals, 15-Minute Action Reviews and Ordered Sharing.

Learning Journals

A Learning Journal is a written log of what you are learning. It provides a point of reference for your ongoing growth of knowledge. It helps you gain some control and insight into how often-subtle changes can make a world of difference. To maintain a Learning Journal, spend between five and ten minutes a day capturing what you have experienced and what you have observed. If you dislike writing, you can draw pictures or use a dictaphone or tape recorder.

Peter Honey, a British consultant and author, suggests the following three-step process when logging your entries:

1. Describe the context of your experience—whether it was good or bad, planned or unplanned. Describe who was involved and how you felt.
2. Summarise your conclusions or lessons learnt from the experiences and dilemmas that you confronted.
3. Develop a plan to do something better or differently in light of your conclusions.

15-Minute Action Reviews

Make 15-Minute Action Reviews part of your daily repertoire. This method has been regularly used in places such as BP–Amoco and the US military for ideas for projects or tasks. The 15-Minute Action Review asks individuals and teams to explore four fundamental questions as they review a task:

1. What was supposed to happen?
2. What actually happened?

3. If there was a difference between what was supposed to happen and what happened, why was there a difference?
4. What can we learn from this?

These conversations can do amazing things to the level of individual, group and business understanding. I use Action Reviews in most of my work when I coach, train or consult. It is particularly valuable when there are clearly observable projects or tasks being undertaken. It also helps in the auditing of processes and in the exploration of why work is being done and how well it is being done.

Ordered Sharing

One of the realities of team or group sharing is that often there are different degrees of vocal contribution. Some people like to verbalise their thinking, while others like to sit quietly. There are numerous times when you will desire people to share their thoughts and feelings on an equal basis. Geoffrey Caine, a US change consultant, introduced the Ordered Sharing method to me in New Zealand a few years ago, and I have been using it ever since.

The reason I find this method so valuable is that it not only helps us to share knowledge, it also builds a sense of community and belonging, which is so vital to fostering trust and support. Further, it helps to create a safe space to share. It is worth noting that Ordered Sharing has very strong parallels to the Open Space technique discussed in Chapter 2 on 'Building trust and support'. The Ordered Sharing process follows four steps:

1. Participants sit in a small closed circle (it usually works best with groups of up to twelve).
2. A question or issue to be explored is selected.
3. Each person expresses an opinion in turn. Listeners must pay full attention, and no one makes any comments on what is being said. The group monitors timing and participation, with each person speaking for 90 seconds. After each person speaks, there is a brief moment of respectful silence before the next person speaks.
4. Having performed the first rotation of conversation, it is often a good idea to revisit the question and ask for further observations about the themes and common messages discussed. This second

exploration helps build threads and shared purpose in what is being communicated.

Like most methods, it will take time for people to feel comfortable with this method. However, after a couple of practices the quality of learning will improve and, most importantly, what really needs to be discussed will be explored. Often this takes the form of a different question or a modified topic.

Mastering your storage and retrieval

In a world of mass information, it is becoming increasingly difficult to remember everything we need to remember. One moment we may feel we are on top of the world in what we need; then all of a sudden we can feel overloaded, smothered and very vulnerable.

During our school days, much emphasis was placed on developing our memory to get us out of trouble by remembering facts, principles and formulas. We may have learnt a variety of techniques, including rote learning, mnemonics or some other technique. Such techniques have been very helpful in the past, but in times of rapid change, we need to go one step further. We need to place greater emphasis on our storage, retrieval and access, rather than relying just on memory. We each need to create systems to recall vital know-how (i.e. principles, stories and facts) at a moment's notice.

We now see this in businesses where archives or databases commonly exist on Help Desks or web pages to point people in the right direction. A common example occurs when we venture into a bank. Depending on what the customer is seeking, the bank employee may follow various on-screen prompts and instructions. They may go to an on-line Help Desk to find the answer. The difficulty arises, however, when the knowledge is not archived and the individual has to use their own resources or memory. This is commonly the case with more complex types of knowledge where a situation is out of the ordinary and has not been documented.

To keep up to date each business needs to make a special effort to keep the right flow of knowledge happening with good storage and exchange methods. For example, information technology platforms such as Lotus Notes allow business people to retrieve and action the latest email and corporate knowledge from their normal work space or on the road. The Australian Bureau of Statistics is one organisation that has built this capability over the last decade.

For the moment, however, let us concentrate on how we can personally store and archive our knowledge. Without a doubt, learning how to archive knowledge has been the turning point in my career. There was a point some years ago when I realised how confused I had become by the mass of information stored in my head and in my office. I was experiencing enormous difficulty keeping track of the resources available to me in the form of office books, notes and files. Then one day, I allocated a proportion of my day to archiving some of the knowledge I had collected. During the following months I built a living archive of my knowledge, in the form of stories, training exercises, latest facts, statistics, best practice organisations, great websites and tips for working smarter.

The result has been truly transformational. Instead of relying on my memory, I now have a system that enables me to retrieve things immediately from my computer. Even when I am tired, or struggling for time, I can in most situations find an answer that has some merit. People often say they are impressed by what I know; but it is not my brilliance or my memory that has made a difference—it is how I store and access my knowledge. This system is simply based on Microsoft Word files and is not sophisticated. In time I will probably create new files using web-browser technology, but for now the system is working. For example, when I decide to do a subject search, I do so by keying in a word or topic and ask the 'find' instruction to retrieve what I have stored. This method has given me instant access to knowledge, which is essential in my profession as a consultant, speaker and author.

The make up of your personal archive will vary depending on your interests. For example, I break my archives into sub-categories to aid prompt access and use. However, there is no need to be too clever; it is more important that the overall structure is simple, flexible and easy to use. As you would expect your archive is never static, and so you will need to update your facts and remove outdated knowledge. I keep a work-in-progress file that has all my latest discoveries; then every three to six months I incorporate these into the main databases. By doing this, I keep the process of maintaining the personal archive manageable and not too time-consuming.

To assist you build your personal archive, here is an alphabetical listing of some possible headings for a personal archive:

- achievements in past jobs and projects
- best practice organisations or better practices you have noticed
- discoveries from your Learning Journal
- distribution lists of important contacts
- excellent contacts (i.e. mentors or advisers or coaches)
- facts, statistics and trends
- favourite quotes
- intranets and databases
- personal mission statement and career goals
- professional associations and personal networks
- references, books and articles
- résumé
- universal wisdom, including key reminders of what is important in your life
- vital procedures and checklists
- websites, e-zines, search engines, interest/discussion groups and learning portals
- wisdom from past training courses and conferences.

Managing your personal knowledge archive is a discipline that gives you the foundation for longevity in your career, while also providing a solid grounding to any hobby or pursuit in life. I have found it to be the best safety valve I could have had in my profession. Of course, there will be times when your archive does not help you or you feel you need a second or third opinion. Perhaps then go to the Internet, or contact someone else for an answer or view. Either way, you cannot lose; you have an archive that will travel with you through life. The latest version of my knowledge archive is on my laptop computer, my office computer and my server so that I can access it at all times wherever I am in the world.

Exploring push and pull technologies

If one is serious about faster and deeper learning, accessing knowledge in the world of digital technology is crucial. In recent years there has been a significant shift in the connectivity and accessibility to the Internet via palmtops and mobile telephone networks in addition to the personal computer. In developed economies the percentage of households with computers is now well over 50 per cent, with additional access also available in other locations such as via digital television, Internet cafes and the workplace. While in developing countries access has historically been very low, it is set to explode in the near future as the cost of wireless mobile devices such as palmtops comes down.

Taking the conversation a little further, it is timely to mention 'push' and 'pull' technologies. In doing so, we are establishing the foundation for a more detailed discussion of digital technology later in this book. In the conversations pertaining to 'growing competitive advantage' we will explore how digital technology can be leveraged for higher levels of learning, customer loyalty and business capability.

Push technologies

Push technologies enable us to be informed about an area of interest when it becomes available. Like getting a letter in the mail, push technologies come in various forms, including voice mail, short message systems, discussion groups, email and electronic newsletters (i.e. e-zines). For me, this means being on the distribution list of various e-zines on topics relevant to winning the knowledge game. These services are often free, but increasingly we are expected to pay for improved knowledge. One site that offers a variety of e-zines is www.austrainer.com.

In a business the idea of push technology can be taken a little further. To aid the flow of vital knowledge, people are often targeted with information based on their speciality, interests and preferences. In the consumer marketplace, intelligent filtering is increasingly being used by businesses such as amazon.com and eBay to influence the future buying decisions of their customers. In the near future push technologies will also extend to 'proximity marketing', where global positioning systems in conjunction with a mobile telephone or palmtop will send us a message based on our geographic location.

Pull technologies

Pull technologies are where we do the searching ourselves and extract the information we need. Search engines are many and varied; I have found of most value www.google.com, www.askjeeves.com and www.dogpile.com. Increasingly businesses now provide sophisticated search capacity to employees, suppliers, strategic alliances and customers to help them find immediate answers, contacts or advice. Here knowledge resources and learning portals are made available to assist suppliers, key customers and employees to do their business. Global organisations like SAP, Cisco Systems and Kodak commonly use their websites as an avenue to inform employees, suppliers and customers on key business operations and new products, as well as sharing important resources such as research, white papers and collaborative opportunities. The premise is that if there is an informed learning business relationship it is a solid one. The media and government bodies at a federal, state or community level are also a wonderful free resource.

There is an assumption, however, that people know how to search the Internet and business websites such as intranets and portals. My experience is that this is often not the case. Very few businesses teach such skills to their employees, suppliers and customers. Greater effort needs to be taken to help people capture simple tips and deeper insights from cyberspace.

Discovering a web of sharers

Learning requires building and nurturing a healthy array of connections, friends and resources. This can rarely be done alone; we all need fellow travellers to help us. For this to happen, we need a spirit that is full of generosity and reciprocity. We need to be generous with our time and energy, and to help others to do the same. Obviously we will find people who do not want to help, and that is to be expected. We also need to accept that some people will need proof of our intentions and desires before they decide to help, particularly given how busy people are in modern living.

To develop a network of sharers, we need to take the lead to show that exchange can be a winning formula. In business, people often make the mistake that this means approaching a senior manager or industry expert, but often the best sources of knowledge may not hold any formal or acknowledged high status position.

So if you wish to build a good network of wisdom in business, you can begin by building a 'Knowledge Map'. This involves continually asking these five questions:

1. Where can I go to find out answers to a process, procedure or way of doing a task base?
2. What information exists in my business and where is it located?
3. What relevant expertise resides outside my business, where does this expertise exist, and how do I gain access to it?
4. What are the best sources of relevant internal and external information?
5. What expertise resides in my business or industry—who knows what?

Creating a Knowledge Map can help you to quickly develop a list of sharers and resources that can help you to explore problems or fill gaps in your learning. You will also soon discover who the real sharers are in business. Then if you are really smart you will make it your business to bring these sharers and opinion leaders together, and put them to work on an important business issue. This is when workplace or industry innovation is at its best.

Summary

The modern business world expects instant answers, action and accountability. However, speed is only part of the equation. We must also learn how to think deeply. Without this capacity we will struggle to make the improvements and progress we need. But we need novel approaches to capturing our wisdom and reviewing progress. It is imperative that we build and maintain a personal and business archive of important contemporary knowledge and contacts. The reality in modern business is that we all need smooth systems to help us quickly access vital sources of enlightenment, inspiration and support. These systems can include keeping Learning Journals, undertaking 15-Minute Action Reviews, participating in Ordered Sharing and establishing Knowledge Maps of important avenues of help and assistance.

CHAPTER 5

Holding meaningful conversations

'Successful knowledge transfer involves neither computers nor documents but rather interactions between people.'—TOM DAVENPORT

Holding meaningful conversations requires:

- teamwork and shared benefit
- trying different processes of group dynamics
- liberating diversity, eccentricity and creativity
- spontaneous exchange and circulation of ideas
- transferring wisdom to where it is most needed.

Inviting a spirit of collaboration

One of the great symbols of freedom is the dove. Seeing one in flight engages many emotions including hope, pride and inspiration. A similar feeling is gained when we share knowledge in meaningful and constructive ways. It lifts our belief that freedom of expression and connection does make a difference. When a conversation works well it provides a level of contribution and collaboration which is very hard to equal. This is because high-leverage knowledge and innovation occurs when people work and learn together. If the flow and exchange is positive, a mutual benefit will result. We may not always be able to measure it, but we do know within the heart when it is happening.

High quality relationships have become the most valuable commodity in business—more important than land, factories and bank accounts. Those who succeed in business today are those who gain the commitment, through partnering and teamwork, of customers, suppliers, alliances and employees. Without this attitude, winning the knowledge game is difficult.

To develop a beneficial relationship, we need to create the right teamwork dynamics. Collaboration can never be taken for granted. It is much more than just communicating or steering a meeting. We need to create maximum opportunities for people to bond, find common ground, establish plans and build on each other's ideas. Without such intention and shared benefit, meaningful conversation will remain a distant dream. Together with a lack of trust, the lack of genuine collaboration is the biggest killer of healthy learning and innovation.

The key to growing successful relationships is not about demanding contribution, it is about both inviting people to participate and then asking for their permission. The more managers impose, the less likely they are to get the openness they need. Forced participation is not only a killer of contribution, it also raises passive resistance, which stifles the potential for quality answers, questions and solutions. To engage higher levels of contribution and collaboration businesses should consider some smart ground rules, which will help guide better exchange and cooperation. By reaching agreement on some commonsense ground rules you will find the group dynamics will be so much easier. The ground rules that I have found most versatile and useful have been adapted from the work of Bob Dick and Tim Dalmau (1999). These are:

- agree on and pursue common goals
- explore why people need each other
- show respect, sharing time and decisions
- attend to each other and listen for understanding
- build on ideas and acknowledge feelings
- reveal assumptions before acting on them
- all take responsibility for the quality of conversation.

Many teams develop their own ground rules. For example, the senior management team at the Centre for Children in the Benevolent Society based in Sydney has developed the following ground rules for being an outstanding team:

- trust, respect and support each other, embracing strengths, experience and diversity
- listen to, communicate with and seek to learn from each other
- have a shared purpose that motivates us
- acknowledge reflection as a vital part of our work
- all take responsibility for the team's effectiveness.

Avoid the trap of going through the motions of being a good team. Come clean on the vital behaviours needed to be truly outstanding and high performing. Build a spirit of collaboration by fostering action and enhanced understanding, while recognising that meaningful conversation is not about ignoring the tough or the difficult issues. It is the exact opposite. We do not want people being so busy being nice that nothing happens. The fact is that when collaboration has purpose and transparency it will contribute more.

We also must encourage people to build on other people's ideas. It is often the case that people loathe using the wisdom of others. According to Korn/Ferry International, an executive recruitment firm that surveyed over 4500 scientists and engineers and 500 corporate leaders, 72 per cent of those surveyed said that knowledge was not reused across their business. Only 12 per cent said they had access to lessons invented elsewhere within their business (Stewart, 2001, p. 203). These results suggest that collaboration is either sadly lacking or poorly channelled in most businesses.

You may want to explore the following questions to raise the standard of collaboration, teamwork and partnering in your own team/s:

- What are the current ways in which people collaborate?
- Which staff, routines and decision-making processes help and hinder collaboration?
- What routines, situations or rituals help people to engage in meaningful conversation?
- Which behaviours or rewards steer people away from meaningful contribution, collaboration and partnering?
- With whom do people collaborate and for what reason?
- Who are the champions and killers of collaboration?

A spirit of collaboration is vital. If there is a feeling of fear or duress, the chances of deep and meaningful conversation will be remote. We need to create healthy dynamics, where people can take responsibility for future action and learning, and be free enough to suggest the radical, wacky and unconventional. Egos can then be tossed out the door and replaced with liberated honesty.

Freshening up your meetings

One of the great throwaway lines in business is: 'We already have knowledge sharing; we hold regular meetings.' As discussed, from experience, such group gatherings are rarely in the knowledge zone; they are full of unspoken agendas, undisclosed ideas and repressed feelings. We need only read the following commonly quoted statistic in the computer industry to understand that we do not always communicate well. It is estimated that 50 per cent of the rework in computer software alone is due to a lack of sharing of assumptions on fundamental issues.

Of course this legacy is not just a bastion of the computer industry. It is a claim that could be made in any area of human communication and interaction. Managers and their businesses generally can do much more to improve the conduct and organisation of interactions, meetings and conversations.

Taking the trouble to review how we meet can make a huge difference to the results we achieve. Over the last twenty years I have made this my speciality, and it never ceases to amaze me what can be generated with a little more imagination, foresight and planning. There are of course times when a firmly controlled agenda and debate are necessary. However, on the whole, this approach is used too often. Creativity and fun cannot be scheduled, but rather need to be engaged and encouraged, with a clear purpose and in the right environment.

There are many ways to freshen up your meetings, ranging from simple adjustments such as having different people chair a discussion to more involved changes such as a high-energy 'idea-jamming' weekend retreat. The key is not to overuse the one technique—mix them around and keep it interesting. In earlier chapters we discussed how methods such as Open Space, 15-Minute Action Reviews and Ordered Sharing can help stimulate innovation and raise awareness. Here are three additional approaches to aid exchange, innovation and learning: Brown-bag Sessions; Knowledge Fairs; and using the Internet.

Brown-bag Sessions

For these sessions, everyone brings their own lunch—hence the word 'brown bag' (or sandwiches can be provided). The topics of these sessions are more far reaching than would be normally discussed at work, and the aim is freewheeling conversations. Examples of topics could be balancing work and home, diet and nutrition or working from home. Often such gatherings include fun and interactive exercises and games. The aim is not heavy and intensive conversation; it is enjoyment, doing something different and building community. It also gives people a chance to explore issues and make connections and friendships that they would not normally do in their work.

Knowledge Fairs

A Knowledge Fair means creating a forum for people to share. They are widely used in businesses and communities across the world. When it comes to Knowledge Fairs the sky is the limit. With the right framework, a little mystery and some celebration, these events can be truly transformational. A successful Knowledge Fair can easily pay for itself in increased enthusiasm, networking and performance for many years to come. Two examples among my clients in the past year have included teams sharing their ideas for better quality in the form of large cardboard posters, and a marketing division of a pharmaceutical company setting up a circus tent in a park and inviting product managers to organise games around product knowledge.

Using the Internet

Meetings and collaborative thinking need not be face to face. Now, with the help of digital technology, ideas can be shared and people can have collaborative experiences in a different time and place. The world of the virtual meeting has truly arrived. Whether you are sharing comments on documents, presentations or emerging thoughts, or using message boards to canvas feedback, being face to face has become less of an issue. We no longer have to be in the same room to begin a meaningful conversation. As long as we have a clear purpose and the right technology we can begin.

To highlight the power of collaborative technology here is one of my favourite stories recounted by Professor Peter Sheldrake from the Royal Melbourne Institute of Technology. He tells the story of a graphic designer in Melbourne who was asked by her manager on a Friday afternoon to complete a newsletter layout by first thing Monday morning. To the manager's complete surprise, the graphic designer completed the job on time. When quizzed on how she did it, she just smiled and said a friend in London helped her by using file sharing and email on her home computer. Further, because of the time difference between London and Melbourne, her friend in London helped on the layout when it was night-time in Australia. (A month earlier, she had done the same in reverse.) This story, which I first heard some five years ago, began my interest in this rapidly growing field. The area of collaborative technology will be explored further in Chapter 11 on 'Leveraging digital technology'.

Getting diverse people together

In many cases, the only way to solve a problem is to get a diverse group of people together. In a 15-minute world, we often do not have the time to wait around; we need to explore new avenues to fast-track thinking and innovation.

To do this we must seek out new ways of promoting a diversity of opinion. In recent years in business we have seen the emergence of many new structures and conversations to do this, including cross-functional teams, scheduled conversations with customers and meetings with suppliers. All these approaches are examples of how businesses are trying to break new ground, open up our minds and discover new learning partnerships. For example, in Sydney, Parramatta City Council, as a result of a management initiative in 2002, established five cross-functional teams to explore better ways of improving organisational capability. This led to new policies, systems and protocols being established, and action plans agreed during the following year.

When viewing this trend we must see it more than just pooling expertise and know-how; we are exploring new ways to help people and business to think differently. As has been said many times before, like-minded people produce like-minded results. So when we are trying to break new ground we can rarely do this by cloning. We need to liberate diversity, eccentricity and creativity to have high-value exchanges and win the knowledge game.

So what does it take to build such positive creative tension? Be assured, fostering different minds to work together is not plain sailing; it can easily raise tension and conflict if not managed properly with the right ground rules. To give some substance to this, let us explore how diversity is managed within new teams, e-teams, and consortiums and joint ventures.

New teams

In any business, hardly a week passes without a team changing shape or a new one forming. When it comes to a new team typically there are a number of priority issues that need to be managed. First of all trust needs to be built and rapport established. One way a new team can do this is to share what they have in common and what special qualities people bring with them to this new experience. A conversation on this may be constructed in a number of ways, including having people explain their current roles and what they hope to do in the new team.

In some cases, it helps to have people tell stories about what they have done in the past. This could include sharing what they feel good about and then following this up with past changes they have made. What are their current interests? What improvements are they now planning? Often you find that these conversations will open up the level of trust and cohesion in the team. Then, having bonded a little, the team is much more likely to work together and resolve the other issues, such as:

- clarifying a common vision and shared purpose
- agreeing on the right behaviours and ground rules
- discussing roles and procedures
- setting up regular rituals for dialogue
- establishing measures for evaluation
- celebrating success.

e-teams

In the modern workplace, it is quite likely that a person will be working with team members who they will never physically meet or are unlikely to do so in the future. In these situations digital technology is the only means of communication, whether it is by the Internet, webcam or videoconferencing. Although the skills of being in an e-team are very similar to that of being in a traditional team, there are some additional challenges that need to be managed.

A firm lesson I have learnt is that in e-team collaboration it is far more difficult to sustain contribution. If deadlines are missed or expectations are not met, people can go missing much faster in e-teams. It is nearly impossible to control behaviour if someone loses interest from 5000 kilometres away. To minimise the risk of this happening, e-teams must nurture wonderful individual effort and deeper thinking by making sure that people work to a planned timetable, agreed purpose and have regular reviews of performance. For the team leader, this means making sure that individual and team effort is rewarded, effort is celebrated and milestones are constantly discussed and reinforced. Again interests can be shared by e-noticeboard technology, which is now freely available in the marketplace.

Consortiums and joint ventures

Managers often pull together talent from other businesses to help generate a stronger collective effort. We see this in many business marketplaces, particularly in welfare, community groups and in small business. For example, in the government or not-for-profit sector, I know of very few agencies and charities that do not pool expertise, resources and costs to work smarter. You also see partnerships in fields such as new high technology, patent development and dot.com ventures, where people pool resources and expertise to better compete with the bigger players in the field. Needless to say it does wonderful things for your reputation and intangible value if you are affiliated or connected to a good group of talent.

Like any form of business partnership, consortiums and joint ventures can raise many issues regarding confidentiality, protection of intellectual property and how the benefits can be rewarded. There is no doubt that if you have different egos, representations or relationships involved in a consortium the process can be more complex. It is fundamentally important to agree on key values, duties and goals. Agreed working behaviours can vary depending on the expectations and history of the people involved, but there needs to be some shared purpose for the consortium to work.

An excellent example is ProGroup, a niche consulting group that specialises in diversity support in the US. ProGroup has modified and updated its listing of behaviours for over five years. By exploring their agreed values listed at www.progroupinc.com you can get some sense of the sorts of issues that can be explored if you venture down the consortium path. The key behaviours of the ProGroup consortium are:

- We are committed to the success of ProGroup and each other.
- We speak positively of our colleagues and clients and treat them with dignity.
- We are responsible for our own well-being and development.
- We listen with respect to each other and to our clients.
- We are a living laboratory and learning organisation.
- We will partner with clients and do our best to identify and address their needs.
- Once we make a commitment, we meet or exceed it.
- We are clear, honest, direct and courageous in all communications.
- We recognise the diversity of ProGroup as a strength to be accepted and appreciated.
- Good intent is assumed and we act in ways that build trust.

- Although we are doing serious work, our workplace will be a positive place where we can be ourselves, laugh and have fun.

Setting up communities of practice

If one chooses to study the human body, we soon discover many amazing things—for example, how the skeleton holds the form and protects the vital organs from harm. Without it, we would immediately fall into a heap of skin and tissue. Also, there are the circulation and nervous systems, which act as our life support and provide trillions of receptors and pathways in our body. They provide the information and fuel we need to survive.

Like the human body, business has its own structure, which gives it its specific shape, look and identity. Like in the human body, the formal reporting structure of a business is supplemented by a circulation system, which helps a business self-organise and adapt. If the circulation system works well, a business will respond in an agile and healthy way. If it fails, the business will struggle to adapt to its own unique environment.

Seeing a business as a living system helps managers and decision makers to better understand how to build different and innovative relationships. Knowledge can be stimulated through a healthy circulation and flow, rather than trying to always resort to control and command. Just as with the human skeleton, a business structure of top-down control is only part of the system we have at our disposal.

Strangely, however, if we try to control the circulation of wisdom in our business we will fail. People are too complex and smart for that management style to work. Most of what happens in business happens informally and out of sight, in private conversations, in tearooms and via email—well beyond the eyes and ears of senior management. The more we try to control or manage knowledge, the less chance we have to put real innovation and change to work. Knowledge has a life force of its own. It has a constant evolution and flow, and we have to tap the informal network as much as possible.

The good news is that there are many examples of organisations exploring and implementing approaches that help knit and blend formal knowledge sharing with the power of informal processes such as the grapevine, chatting and spontaneous exchange. One approach is called 'communities of practice'. Other labels for this method include cross-functional teams, cross-boundary groups, communities of experience, and interest or discussion groups. Of course the label or term does not matter. What is more important is that what is generated frees up the level of know-how and stimulates cross-fertilisation of ideas. In time the business benefits either directly or indirectly.

The effectiveness of communities of practice has also been backed up with solid evidence. Harkins, Carter and Timmins (2000), who edited a study of best practice knowledge management, found that building communities was a major driver in the success of knowledge-creation strategies. Other success factors included having a sharper business focus, a total commitment at all levels of the organisation, and, finally, having adequate rewards and incentives.

Some examples of communities of practice include:

- The Australian Human Resources Institute (AHRI) has established and supported special interest groups for its members on specialist subject areas for well over a decade.
- The Department of Defence in New South Wales established a network of seventy-five training liaison officers in the 1980s to better share resources and ideas on learning and development.
- The New South Wales Department of Health established learning pathways across regions to explore high priority health issues among professionals.
- A pharmaceutical business established study groups to explore solutions to a number of pressing issues, including customer data management and knowledge management. The groups were cross-functional and included senior, middle and junior staff.
- Ernst & Young has over twenty-two global networks supporting the development of their organisational archive of knowledge.
- Shell has funded well over 150 communities of practice. One example is where instrumentation engineers network with each other to solve technical problems across the world.
- Xerox technicians meet informally at the end of each day to share stories about what is happening in the field.

Finally, it is worth noting that a vibrant and successful community of practice needs to be a worthwhile contributor to the business. To be successful a healthy community of practice will most likely have:

- a common sense of purpose, within the broad expectations of a business
- the desire to share knowledge and self-manage itself
- a high level of trust and loyalty
- a common digital technology system, which enables easy communication and connection
- a highly respected and visible leadership, which refrains from dominating proceedings
- adequate budgets and administrative support
- positive mentoring, coaching and peer support
- the chance for deeper and more confidential advice outside the pry of public scrutiny
- a passion and commitment with good facilitation
- realistic expectations about its purpose
- if the time comes for closing up or disbanding that is seen as OK.

Circulating wisdom

Without the circulation of wisdom, great initiatives such as exciting team meetings and communities of practice may never reach their full potential. Again, there are numerous ways to circulate wisdom within a business. The path you choose depends in part on the style and character of the knowledge involved. Simple checklists or routines can be shared if they are written down, but when the wisdom is locked up in people's minds in the form of stories or experience they are harder to use. Great care must be taken to give the time for people to share their formulas, mental models and views of the world.

Here are some examples of how knowledge can be generated and dispersed successfully in business:

- A team applies their newly learnt knowledge to a new situation or scenario. For example, a sales team reviews their performance and applies what they have learnt to the following week's activities.
- Individuals and groups archive what they have learnt, and place it on a business database so that it can be used by others.
- People provide peer assistance to another team. For example, a team leader in a factory in Fiji has developed a new way of reducing toxic waste. The global head office in Paris hears of this, and the

Fijian team leader is asked to go to Mexico to help reduce toxic waste in another factory. The team leader's job is to get the Mexican team thinking, by listening and asking questions and avoiding telling them what is required. The Fijian team leader returns with new knowledge discovered in Mexico, and makes further changes in Fiji.

- Scenarios, work in progress or case studies are placed on a business website or discussion forum to get other people's opinions. This is particularly valuable in regard to situations that are yet to be confronted, or for those challenges that are more complex. For example, a past CEO of Heinz Watties in New Zealand described how he established shadow executive meetings of junior staff to review situations that were explored by senior executives at another time.
- For those very infrequent requests such as obsolete technology and unique processes, a person is appointed to monitor and make sure the question is answered. In larger organisations good digital technology is important and on many occasions people may need to raise their question/s on the Internet to get the result they are seeking.

Summary

Generating excellent collaboration requires excellent communication, cohesive purpose and creative thinking with the right people at the right time and for the right reason. In this regard, having meaningful opportunities to participate is vitally important. Examples include: cross-functional teams, e-teams and communities of practice. Businesses are full of innovative and fresh approaches to interaction and cross-fertilisation. However, just because people are communicating or having a meeting does not necessarily mean they are experiencing winning innovation and business thinking. The ultimate success lies in the flexibility of leadership and the ability to ignite interest and involvement. Only then will there be opportunities to open people's hearts and minds, thereby establishing the fertile ground needed to grow competitive advantage and ensure lasting success.

PART 2

Growing competitive advantage

To achieve competitive advantage in business requires a careful blend of excellent leadership, smart digital technology and inspired contribution from a wide range of people. Business success relies on a combination of factors that are tightly related to how well know-how is shared and put to work. For this to happen, a business culture must be grown that rewards the smart use of talent while also protecting vital secrets. There is no single path or quick fix solution. You need to keep an eye on a variety of targets, including smart business discipline, fostering an attitude of sharing, being adaptable to change, sustaining and keeping talent, leveraging digital technology, increasing customer loyalty and providing a rich array of opportunities for learning and innovation.

CHAPTER 6

Creating a smarter business

'If Hewlett Packard knew what Hewlett Packard knows, we would be three times more profitable.'
—LEW PLATT

Creating a smarter business requires:

- both business intelligence and counterintelligence
- marketplace data and research from private and public sources
- clear and powerful direction from top management
- focusing attention on learning hot spots
- championing sharing and innovation efforts.

Being on the cutting edge

The good news in twenty-first century business is that you do not have to have a big bank account to be rich in knowledge and be competitive. A little ingenuity can go a long way. In the knowledge era, know-how and ingenuity have become the major barometer for national, regional and business wealth. In most developed economies the majority of wealth is now in the form of human capital, intellectual capital and talent, rather than physical capital such as plant and equipment. Knowledge, and being on the cutting edge, is without doubt the key competitive advantage, not only for the private sector but for all forms of government and community-based organisations.

The benefits of creating a smarter business can be vast. Benefits can include superior insight into customer behaviour, more finely tuned service delivery and repeat business. Further, a better understanding of the marketplace and trends ensures an improved cycle of innovation and operational efficiency through a more responsive decision-making process. This enhances your ability to be successful through the better use and mix of talent, intellectual capital and customer relationships. This normally translates into a business model where you are doing things better, faster and cheaper.

In saying this it is understandable why creating a smarter business through a better use of knowledge and innovation does not happen naturally. It is not an easy task to set the agenda overnight. Even a seasoned decision maker or manager can struggle as they try to make sense of what needs to be done. However, from observing the field for over a decade, I believe there are some basic principles that can help in this endeavour.

To start with, good implementation has less to do with cash flow and budgets and more to do with enterprise and clear thinking. You need to be acutely aware of your business, its operating environment and how you rate in the delivery of service and product performance. The bottom line may be different between corporate, government and community businesses, but the need for honest assessment of performance and how you position your knowledge does not diminish. Every business plan needs to deliver a healthy balance of responsiveness and pragmatic action.

Creating a business requires a special brand of leadership that continually reminds people of the value of knowledge, while making it easier for them to do their job and make a worthwhile contribution. Just telling them to be smarter or more creative will drive them crazy unless you back it up with the right procedures, methods and processes. In some cases you may need to appoint people to be specialists in the roles of competitive intelligence, knowledge creation and talent management, but more often than not you will need to foster a business culture and attitude that means everyone sees these outcomes as part of their everyday job.

Needless to say, the leadership of senior management is paramount. To win the knowledge game, managers need to be much less concerned with cost savings, risk minimisation and the bottom line, and be more concerned with the smart use of knowledge, deeper thinking and better application. Winning the knowledge game needs a sharp focus, people who are motivated to participate, systems and infrastructure that are user-friendly. Whatever the state of the economy and your current cycle of business, know-how is the only thing that will help you move forward.

In this regard, all businesses need to continually explore three cutting edge questions:

1. What are the current capabilities of the business/organisation?
2. What issues will face the business in the immediate future (say two years)?
3. What are the gaps in your capabilities and what needs urgent attention?

The suggested two-year time frame may be too short in some markets, while in others it may be too long. Your experience is important here. The key to sustaining excellence is patient, strategic and careful intelligence, rather than relying on luck.

Being on the cutting edge requires that different parts of the business are talking and collaborating. Teamwork is everything; you need to organise well-designed consultation and feedback processes so that the latest trends on marketing research, customer satisfaction and business planning are in the engine room of the 'business brain'.

Here are some examples of how smart observation has helped some businesses stay at the cutting edge and in tune with their marketplace:

- a sales representative noticed a competitor had changed their super-market product-stacking strategy and discussed it back in the office
- a health-care organisation discovered a recent government study on world trends in hospital infections, which found a statistically significant increase in infections in the previous twelve months
- an independent study of the mobile telephone industry discovered that lead times to answer customer calls were worse than those of its two major competitors
- a government employee discovered that the funding for their department was likely to be cut by 10 per cent in the next financial year
- a business developed a list of website addresses that gave them a quick weekly scan of their environment, including competitors, existing and potential partners, suppliers, customers and opinion leaders.

Managers also need to ensure there is adequate security and counter intelligence. PricewaterhouseCoopers estimated in 1999 that theft of intellectual property cost Fortune 1000 companies $US45 billion per annum (West, 2001, p. 184). It is imperative to have a risk management strategy to defend your trade secrets and proprietary knowledge. This will be explored in much more depth in Chapter 10 on 'Protecting intellectual property'. However, for now, we need to consider what security audits and system checks may be necessary in your business. These may include limiting availability of sensitive knowledge, screening sensitive conversations, briefing key personnel on security issues, knowing how to handle the media, and being prepared to establish confidentiality agreements with your business partners.

When it comes to competitive intelligence, a clear policy is imperative. For example, such a policy might explain ethical and legal practice, and how people can make a contribution to the 'business brain'. Input can be helped by producing an easy-to-use system, which includes simple work sheets that can be completed either on paper or in digital form, rewards for contributions and the coordination of ideas on key issues. Remember though that knowledge can be inaccurate, biased or late—so make sure you always double-check your facts. In some cases, you may find it easier to outsource competitive intelligence to an external provider. However, be careful, as often a third party may not have a good understanding of your business, or you might lose benefits of cost savings and objectivity.

Sources of competitive intelligence

Most businesses are quite unsophisticated when it comes to gathering competitive intelligence. Research from the Society of Competitive Intelligence Professionals and Professor Chris Hall at Macquarie University confirms this is the case, particularly for small to medium-sized businesses, which often rely on a small circle of trusted contacts, magazines or newspapers to grow their view of the marketplace.

So what can you do? Depending on available time, desire and motivation, there are many sources of competitive intelligence. The good news is that much of what you need is free and in the public domain, in the form of reports and studies. There is also a host of technology tools, which can help you understand your business, while also providing database access to information, literature searches and analysis. Below is a summary of some of the sources of competitive intelligence, ranging from simple access to government and industry websites that are in the public domain to holding private conversations with competitors.

Public domain

Irrespective of your business there is business intelligence information that can help you. Examples include:

- directories, including books such as *The Almanac of Business and Industrial Financial Ratios*, and on-line services such as Business Information on the Internet (www.rba.co.uk/sources/index.htm), the Thomas Register (www.thomasregister.com) and the Dow Jones Interactive Web Center available for subscription at www.dowjones.com
- market research companies, which can provide data on consumer perceptions, retail outlets, brands and distribution, sales, customer satisfaction, mystery shopping, product image and service quality assessment
- development applications for buildings and extensions to sites
- patent, trademark and intellectual property information
- public information from businesses themselves—for example, company brochures, annual reports, company accounts, catalogues,

buying directories, house journals and newsletters, news releases, web pages, executive speeches and information from trade shows
- reports, such as those from securities and exchange agencies, federal, state and local government, business councils, chambers of commerce, investment companies (e.g. Merrill Lynch), rating services companies (e.g. Moody's), credit reports (e.g. Dun & Bradstreet), professional or industry associations, professional publications, business newspapers, local community publications, market research reports, university reports and lobby or pressure groups
- the Internet, including discussion groups, portals and corporate attack sites.

In doing competitive intelligence in the public domain you may discover that much of the information you find already exists internally, particularly if you belong to a medium to large business. Always do a competitive intelligence audit of your internal sources of competitive intelligence first to ensure you are not reinventing the wheel. You may be surprised at how much useful data is already lying around gathering dust in the form of printed reports, computer files and other studies.

With the emergence of search engines on the Internet, searching of public information has become so much easier. However, be careful, as much of what is on the Internet lacks independent review and credibility. In some cases you may decide to pay to get the best and most reliable information. Fee-paid services are increasingly being provided by organisations such as Reuters, Associated Press, Dun & Bradstreet and ACNielsen to name a few.

Private domain

Having explored the public domain, it is also important to converse with those people who can give you the most precise and powerful intelligence on your marketplace or business. Talking to staff, customers and contacts in the field is a prime example. Often this form of intelligence is not on the public record, but the insights gained can be very valuable. Private comments and disclosures can come from a variety of sources. You may have people who can help you within your business. However, remember a person's opinion can be prone to error—so tread carefully. To gain the best value you will need careful training, briefing and reporting systems.

Ethics are very important too, and of course always avoid theft, bribery or misrepresentation. For example, how would you approach a person now working with you who had in the past worked for a competitor? How would you frame the conversation so that it is ethical, lawful and would not cause harm or compromise the person? Revisit the code of practice from the Society of Competitive Intelligence Professionals and the 'gut test' detailed in the introduction to this book. This will help your business respond better to any ethical dilemmas you may face.

Typically the most accurate sources of private domain knowledge are employees, suppliers or customers working within the business under study. Always ensure that the conversation is non-threatening and does not place them in a difficult situation. Be transparent, keep it simple and do not ask for highly confidential and precise information. Often people will reveal vital information anyway, which is not seen as confidential, particularly when they feel the exchange is one of mutual benefit. It is better to have your contacts giving approximations and generalisations, rather than forcing unlawful disclosures. Always be prepared in advance—this form of intelligence gathering takes tremendous skill and practice to perfect.

Other sources of external private domain research could involve contacting journalists, former employees, other players in the marketplace, such as competitors and consultants, and many of the people who are listed in the public domain categories, such as those working with professional associations and market research companies.

Communicating your direction for knowledge work

Apart from being aware of competitive intelligence and what it takes to be on the cutting edge, it is imperative that you establish an engaging and powerful argument for change. This articulation helps set a target in which people can organise and tailor their behaviour, priorities and learning. How you choose to tell your story or direction will depend to a large extent on the personality and receptiveness of your people.

Discussed next are three approaches to communicating your direction: articulating priority business needs; communicating a vision of the future; and describing unacceptable behaviours. The final choice or mix will depend on the nature of your business and how you can grab and hold people's attention.

Articulating priority business needs

One popular way of communicating direction is for leaders and decision makers to articulate their priority business needs. The benefit of doing this is that it gives a sharp focus for knowledge work and innovation. As you would expect, the measures can be very idiosyncratic, depending on the business. In a public health business such as a hospital, the needs could be as simple as saving lives. Or they could be achieving a better response to patient needs, minimising infection or helping patients feel a little less lost in the system.

Likewise, if you were studying an international consulting organisation such as Ernst & Young, the drivers for improved knowledge work might include the smarter use of existing knowledge, improved customer satisfaction, and attracting and keeping talent. Other common business measures include:

- increased productivity and profitability
- reduced time for a product or service to enter the marketplace
- reduced wastage, error and duplication
- greater social responsibility, duty of care and environmental management
- stronger alliances and relationships with business partners.

There is a further discussion on the measurement and evaluation of knowledge in Chapters 14 and 15.

Communicating a vision of the future

The second way of helping shape a direction for knowledge work and innovation is to communicate a vision of the future. Here you develop a story of what your future would look like if you were acting as a smarter business. The two examples below, from Buckman Laboratories and Hewlett Packard, show how a short story can have enormous impact. In both cases, the visions have had a profound and lasting impact on how these businesses have progressed in the area of knowledge work over the past decade.

In 1988 Bob Buckman, the CEO at Buckman Laboratories, provided a template for the future of the business by spelling out what he was expecting in the area of cutting-edge knowledge work. He wanted a system and knowledge management practice that met the following criteria:

- It would be possible for people to talk to each other directly to minimise distortion.
- It would give everyone in the company access to the company's knowledge base.
- It would allow each individual in the company to enter the knowledge into the system.
- It would be available twenty-four hours a day, seven days a week.
- It would be easy to use.
- It would communicate in whatever language is best for the user.
- It would be updated automatically; capturing questions and answers as a future knowledge base.

Within a division of Hewlett Packard, the senior leadership of their consulting team developed this vision:

> Our consultants feel and act as if they have the knowledge of the entire organisation at their fingertips when they consult with the customers. They know exactly where to go to find information. They are eager to share knowledge as well as leveraging others' experience in order to deliver more value to customers. We will recognise those consultants who share and those who leverage others' knowledge and experience as the most valuable members of the HP team.

Both of these case studies provide a structure by which people can shape their behaviour.

Describing unacceptable behaviours

The third approach to shaping the direction for knowledge and innovation is quite different. Here you describe the behaviours that are no longer acceptable. This sets in place a criterion or benchmark for monitoring unsatisfactory performance, particularly if backed up with appropriate reward and recognition systems that encourage better behaviour. A list of undesirable behaviours could include:

- great ideas not being shared with the people who matter
- mistakes being repeated because they are not recorded and learnt from in the first place
- vital knowledge being stored by too few people
- critically important wisdom being lost when employees leave the business
- people struggling to find out what is known in the business, and being unable to plan
- limited opportunities to share wisdom across the business
- no innovation, training and skill development
- control and command dominates
- poor customer relations
- sales are always won by dropping the price.

Having identified unacceptable behaviours, you are then much better placed to undertake regular reviews in shifts in performance levels to measure improvement, deterioration or the status quo. Here testimonial quotes can also be a wonderful supplement to the review. Real-life testimonials or narrative stories can give enormous weight and substance that positive change may be occurring. This process of digging up the real life proof will be explored more in the next chapter on 'Spreading a knowledge-sharing virus'.

Knowing the learning hot spots

If the central message in this chapter were to be summarised, it is that creating a smarter business requires quality business intelligence, observation of performance and clear direction. If your business does this well, you are much more likely to identify the important hot spots or areas for knowledge improvement. Then as each hot spot is addressed, the business can move on to the next issue, and so on.

Clearly if you wish to get individual 'buy in', the business must communicate why addressing these hot spots is important. People must see learning about hot issues as meaningful, real and important work. You need to grab their attention, by stimulating curiosity. On a personal level you may need to stress the benefit of working and learning about these issues. Other personal benefits may involve enhancing people's reputation, employability, feeling acknowledged, developing mutual respect and making people look good. Likewise you may also link the broader benefits to the business, customer or society. The benefits can be both large and diverse.

The key here is maximising contribution to knowledge and learning; it is not about living out a prison sentence. Forced contribution has a very low success rate, as well as generating hostility or passive resistance. Go for short bursts of innovation rather than long and protracted involvement.

As discussed in Chapter 4, depth of thinking is also vitally important. Encourage people to keep journals and contribute to archives of knowledge on the hot issues under investigation. If you have access to digital technology, use it to encourage people to answer and help each other. For example, instead of having vital people spending hours proofreading and editing text, get others to help them to do this task. Remember though to gain their permission, trust and goodwill. If you face resistance from people, try exploring the following questions to increase involvement and assistance:

- Do you know why this issue is so important and what it involves?
- Do you know how easy it is to help?
- What needs to change in order for you to contribute more?
- What other issues need to be discussed first, before you are ready to commit?
- What happened last time you tried to share or contribute?
- What could we do more of to encourage you to participate differently?
- What are you concerned about losing if you share or contribute?
- What would you see are the benefits of sharing or contributing more?
- Are you prepared or interested in being part of the solution?

You will find these questions help clarify misunderstandings as well as helping to surface hidden tensions or concerns. You may also need to conduct formal training and coaching sessions that clearly demonstrate the merits of sharing knowledge and its potential for both individual and business benefit. Of course when you design the training make sure it embodies the principles of knowledge sharing and celebration, as opposed to a strict formal lecture where the opposite dynamics are often the case.

Gluing the lessons together

Here is a list of eleven observations to help summarise the topic area as well as serving as a precursor to various discussions that will unfold in remaining chapters:

1. Creating a smarter business requires total commitment. In most cases the impetus for change comes from a recognition that the competition or business landscape has moved on. Through closer scrutiny of customer relationships, industry trends and early warning signals, a business has a much better chance of responding.
2. Each manager needs to champion the flow of ideas. When key findings of know-how are discovered, important decisions must be shared in a timely, credible and ethical way, without hurting the business. Normally this means ensuring key messages are clearly communicated to help understanding, application and review.
3. People need to be convinced that both the individual and the business will benefit from winning the knowledge game. People are too busy to be sidetracked to do meaningless activity. Take the mystery out of such terms as knowledge management, learning organisations and business excellence, and create maximum opportunity for learning on the job.
4. Effective implementation occurs by focusing effort on a few hot learning topics rather than trying to do too much. Make sure you are supporting and nurturing discovery and innovation in these areas. Then ensure that the learning is captured and shared with the right people at the right time.
5. Information technology must be about connecting people. Chatting by email or having a meeting on the Internet does not automatically mean you have knowledge sharing. You need to make sure good ideas are put into practice.
6. People must understand that they need each other and that sharing of knowledge expands possibilities. People should be encouraged to set up informal discussion groups to exchange lessons learnt and tricks of the trade.

7. Sharing stories is central to growing know-how and business capacity. Actively encourage people to share testimonials, stories and observations at every opportunity, whether it is coaching or leading a meeting. It is here where deeper insight and awareness is unmasked.
8. Management technologies and analytical tools are also of great assistance in winning the knowledge game. Popular models used extensively in business include the Balanced Scorecard (Kaplan and Norton, 1996), Business Excellence Frameworks and Six Sigma (Harry and Schroder, 2000).
9. Every knowledge exchange needs to be prepared for and reflected upon; success does not happen by accident. Encourage collaboration and teamwork. You can even consider redesigning your physical workspace to encourage greater sharing and openness.
10. When you are struggling for talent in your business, look for innovative ways to build your capability. These include buying in expertise, hiring new employees and forming joint ventures. Similarly, seeking help from consultants, suppliers and industry associations could be a sensible way of proceeding.
11. Consider incentive plans to encourage people to create and apply their knowledge. Some workplaces link knowledge management into their performance management agreements, while others reward the knowledge sharers and innovators by inviting them to special events or gatherings. Most of all, get the message out that you are serious about winning the knowledge game.

Summary

Creating a smarter business requires a careful understanding of your marketplace, environment and performance. To do this you need a clever combination of intelligence gathering and security. Clear goals can then be set, and your direction modified if necessary. It can all then be glued together with a common infrastructure, incentives to share knowledge and a clear focus on the hot issues that will help drive and grow your competitive advantage. There is no single solution. You will need to deploy a range of consistent and aligned strategies over time to succeed.

CHAPTER 7

Spreading a knowledge-sharing virus

'We don't see knowledge management as a technology issue; we see it as something that needs to be part of how we work in every different aspect of the firm.'—STEPHANIE PURSLEY

Spreading a knowledge-sharing virus requires:

- much higher levels of cooperation
- personalising a word-of-mouth campaign
- less fuzzy rhetoric and more real-life examples
- balancing the conflicting needs of security and freedom
- digging out the unsaid and unspoken forms of wisdom.

Stimulating a team approach

Businesses are inherently political in nature; they are full of people seeking to serve their own agendas, views and needs. Sometimes business politics can help growth and success, but more often than not it causes the opposite—people spend more time infighting and protecting territory than sharing ideas and growing capability. In many ways one could easily argue that winning the knowledge game has more to do with handling business politics than with being at the forefront of best practice. Businesses are highly political in nature, and there is a strong connection between political influence, power and the flow of knowledge.

So how should we respond to business politics? One positive way is to view politics as a natural part of life. We may not necessarily like what we experience, but instead of being paralysed by what we see, we need to invest in more creative ways to inspire people to try different codes of behaviour, with the aim of raising the levels of teamwork and shared purpose. We may not be able to easily change the psyche of people, but we can skilfully raise another view, which could lead to different habits being entrenched and the spreading of a knowledge-sharing virus.

It needs to be accepted that people will always bring to the table widely different motivations, mental models and assumptions. For example, with learning and innovation there is a wide array of perceived benefits. Senior management may view the growing of knowledge as a strategic issue—one that needs organisation-wide commitment. Employees on the other hand may view knowledge as something that gives them personal recognition or helps them to do their job. A specialist in information technology may be motivated by an entirely different value system, such as one involving the implementation of the very latest communication and digital technology capabilities. Alternatively, a human resources practitioner may be more interested in issues such as training support, resistance to change and consultation rather than a pure technology-based solution. With such diversity of opinion it is very easy to see where the many sources of political tensions and agendas can arise. Left unchecked, different views can quickly paralyse any change effort. Of course such tribal wars are not restricted to these professions and roles. There is often baggage that comes with the territory, whether it is indoor versus outdoor staff, head office staff versus regional office staff, or the common divisions between finance and marketing, or research and development and manufacturing.

To create a team effort, high levels of cooperation must be stimulated. You need to move past egos including your own and pull together in one direction for any change to succeed. You do not want people looking for the exit row and escaping when things get tough. To remove mystery and suspicion there must be easy and safe ways for people to contribute. Time needs to be given to clear up expectations and find a common language. Ignoring political conflict will not help; you need to be courageous enough to get the parties together and look for common ground. This advice also applies to relationships with suppliers, consultants, vendors, joint venture partners and customers. It is imperative that the right mix of representation occurs, especially in a topic like winning the knowledge game where so many people can have a stake in its success.

Seven behaviours that can improve your chances of political cooperation are:

1. Never assume you have common ground; work hard for a shared purpose.
2. Encourage people to say what they are thinking in safety.
3. Promote fluid and spontaneous exchange of ideas.
4. Remind people that if they think they know it all, they are kidding themselves.
5. Support people to hang in there, even when things become heated or they feel hurt.
6. Make sure people are involved in important decision making and clarification.
7. Continually reward and thank people for their efforts, without patronising them.

Of course such teamwork will not come easily; it requires leadership and skilful facilitation that sparks people into action by unleashing spirit, passion and the desire to contribute. At higher levels of cooperation people are required to challenge their assumptions, and listen to each other—and that is often not easy. Similarly, if a department or professional wants to take governance or control over a change this must be discussed.

Shaping public opinion

How well you shape public opinion and word of mouth will ultimately determine whether you will gain commitment to any change. This is particularly the case in knowledge and innovation. People need to personally understand why and how better knowledge adds value. Relying solely on logic and economic argument is not enough. People need to experience a meaningful exchange, which stimulates higher levels of trust and makes them feel vitally important. A common area where this does not happen is between a manager and their staff. Unless the manager coaches with a genuine desire to build talent for mutual benefit, the relationship will soon lose impetus. All the words in the world will not make a scrap of difference if the heart is not there. Relying on correction, control and micro-management is a sure recipe for turning off the flow of knowledge in any manager–staff relationship. So be ready for change yourself if you are going to have a positive impact on public opinion.

A much better way is to earn people's respect and commitment. Managers need to recognise that it is not something you can impose or conscript—you need people to volunteer both their time and their interest. If a business is only out to benefit its own cause, people will quickly see through this and resist. Unless you lead from the heart and seek to address areas of mutual need you will struggle to progress in stimulating improved knowledge, innovation and performance. This lesson of leadership is relevant to any form of human interaction, but it is especially so in business.

So avoid waging a war against an entrenched culture and bruised egos. You need to build a partnership where the business conditions make it easier for people to contribute, be listened to and valued. In the world of dealing with human emotion, reputation, promises and loyalty mean nothing if you are not backing this up with a genuine desire to be helpful, fair and transparent.

From a CEO perspective you certainly need to keep an eye on the budget and ensure efficient allocation of resources, but you must also be prepared to champion the cause of circulation and application of talent. Growing competitive advantage is about helping people to find out what needs to be developed, learnt and thrown out to make it easier for them to get on with the job in a smarter way.

If working together comes down to who is right and who is wrong, you will only sow the seeds for discontent, token compliance and hostility. Gaining commitment and shaping public opinion takes time. It is not a single one-stop solution. Be prepared for a pursuit that will require a diversity of tactics and ideas. Whether you are aiming to gain big leaps in support, or you are following a more cautious approach, be prepared for a journey full of surprises, intrigue and great learning.

To help shape public opinion ensure:

- a clear and compelling case for change is sold
- people are involved in meaningful dialogue
- mistakes are learnt from rather than jumping to punishment
- people feel appreciated and know how to contribute
- prime examples of good knowledge work are rewarded and marketed
- there is a development focus that supports and encourages learning
- progress is continually reviewed and celebrated.

Also develop the skill of personalising word-of-mouth and marketing campaigns to different audiences. For example, for the more innovative people in your business you may need to highlight how a proposed change is fresh, ground breaking and will help them stay ahead of the pack. Others will require clear proof that an idea has merit before they are prepared to commit themselves. They also may want to know that it is practical, achievable and user friendly before they will give you their time and effort. Finally you may need to convince others of the potential loss if they fail to grab the opportunity. Having clear demonstrations of tried and true methods certainly helps, particularly if it is backed up with proof that others are already benefiting.

Such a range of possible messages highlights how important it is to sell the benefits in a careful way. This means positioning your message in less abstract, risky or complex terms. Sometimes the obvious is much better than the cute. For example, credible testimonials and stories on what is now working, or what has worked in the past, can often help sway public opinion in a positive direction.

Most of all, support people to explore their options and consider alternatives in safety without fear or retribution. In doing so you will increase the chances of surfacing the hidden fears or tensions that may be consuming them. From there you are much better placed to move forward together.

We also must be sensitive to the fact that people are often more emotionally connected and loyal to their work groups or teams than to the business. For many, the concept of what makes up the identity and boundaries of your business is a very abstract or hard-to-connect-to concept. People are more likely to be loyal to those in their work team or department, particularly in medium to large businesses. Loyalty is more likely to be a group thing, rather than one in which people feel obligated to a total business or workplace. If you expect loyalty you will need to convince people that not only are they going to benefit as individuals but also the team in which they work will also see a reward.

To help explore resistance to change, here is a series of questions you may wish to consider when holding your next conversations:

- What is your understanding of what is happening at this time?
- What is your past experience of such initiatives?
- How hopeful are you that this change will be a success?
- Why do you believe this change is seen as important?
- What do you fear if you try this change?
- What are the advantages or disadvantages of this change?
- What do you think I need to understand about your views on this matter?
- How can we work better on this together?

Digging up the best proof

If you want to accelerate acceptance and buy-in to winning the knowledge game managers and their businesses need to dig up proof. We need to steer clear of fuzzy rhetoric and jargon, and paint a vivid picture of what is possible. The best way to do this is to share a story or a testimonial that attaches some meaning to what is required. Avoid abstract concepts and provide concrete examples.

Stephen Denning (2000) in his book *The Springboard* discusses how in the World Bank he shared stories to help create a knowledge-focused organisation. He found that sharing short narrative stories helped people to quickly relate to what is being said or proposed. One of Denning's popular stories started with the following words:

In June 1995, a health worker in Kamana, Zambia, logged on to the CDC website in Atlanta and got the answer to a question on how to treat malaria…

This short story about what a person actually did provided a powerful mental framework for decision makers and staff on what knowledge sharing is all about. It also gave listeners the freedom to explore countless possibilities in their own minds on what this story meant to them and how it could be applied. For example, Denning discussed how a person might reflect on the health worker story:

> Suppose I was part of such a network of like-minded and sharing professionals. Suppose that I had access to such a service. I could be more productive. I could help my clients and provide faster, better services. I would have a solution. Suppose…

Taking Denning's advice a little further, such proof can provide the evidence that a new or different way of doing something is not only possible, it is already happening. It also provides a catalyst for deeper exploration and insight into possible consequences and benefits of change.

So if you have not done so already, start collecting stories of real people and real situations, and use them to support a change or a new way of thinking. Also as you walk around the business or connect with people, make a careful note of what is being said, what is being learnt and what assumptions are being generated. Use personal accounts and testimonials where you can. Better still, encourage people to tell their own story in public or in the right marketing campaign. Such evidence can add enormous credibility to any change process. You will soon discover that well-chosen case studies and stories will not only spark interest, they will also help shape public opinion. People will begin to see how the future or the current realities could be shaped differently, without their egos being dented or their image being tarnished.

The beauty of stories is that they are quick and easy to use. As Stephen Denning points out, people do not need a long detailed explanation; all they need is a short narrative to get them thinking. Most people will have many stories already, so why not place a series of thirty-word narratives in a personal archive for future use. When prompted, tell more about the meaning and message behind the story.

Of course, storytelling is not foolproof. Stories can go astray, particularly if you fail to consider the needs of the audience and the key message you are trying to convey. So rehearsal and prethinking is essential, and with a little intrigue and good timing people are more likely to tune in. When it comes to storytelling you may not be able to control where they go in their own minds—so take the time to explore the observations, conclusions or thinking that have been generated. Then you will not only be generating more curiosity and attention, you will also be taking everyone's learning to a new and different place.

Keeping the electricity flowing

The greater our ability to generate a flow of ideas within a network of sharers, the greater the potential for breakthrough thinking. Being isolated and alone in the twenty-first century knowledge era is a sure recipe for business stagnation. We must be clear on how our behaviour impacts on others, and how the knowledge-sharing virus grows. For example, when we turn on the flow of electricity in our home, the divide between what is on and off is very stark. Similarly the on/off switch for the flow of knowledge sharing is equally stark and self-evident. Depending on how we lead, coach and manage, a manager can stimulate flow or can cut it off at a moment's notice. So remember the on/off switch and respect the needs and motivations of others.

Here again, let us remind ourselves of some of the principles already discussed. If we wish to promote sharing of knowledge, the business needs to radiate trust and receptivity. Knowledge work needs to be encouraged as a normal part of daily activity, and not an extra thing to do at the end of the day. We need to agree on goals and identify hot issues that need attention and give people meaning. It needs to be planned for and rewarded. Most of all we need to be respectful of people's time and effort, whatever the outcome. In times of such rapid change, there is a multitude of reasons why people may choose not to share their knowledge and we need to understand that—before trying to force participation. My sense is that most people already know deep down what it takes to share, but they rarely talk about it. If you build a track record of being a knowledge sharer, you will find the right connections in time. In doing so, you will also earn vital respect and integrity by being grateful of people's time and effort.

As will be discussed in Chapter 11, information technology is also a great help in opening up new networks and building a spirit of collaboration and sharing. However, technology by itself is not the answer; it is just the mechanism and a tool. We need to back up the technology with human processes, which personalise relationships and make people feel valued and appreciated. When this occurs we have the best of both worlds—one in which there is an ease of communication and frequent exchange.

Finally, to keep the electricity flowing, be respectful of how people feel about their personal security and freedom. If either is under threat, people may withdraw and resist any new requests. So be aware that if people feel their future is threatened they will most likely choose not to help out. Such a perceived or possible threat may need to be acknowledged or discussed before any progress can be made.

Turning silver into gold

Our knowledge is wired in context and experience. Just because someone is successful in one business venture does not mean they will automatically be successful again or continue to succeed in their present situation. Our ability to resolve something depends to a very large extent on our ability to apply the right learning and insight to the right situation.

This quirky relationship between context and our knowledge poses fascinating questions about how we change our habits, grow our experience and expand our know-how. Firstly, how skilful are we at exploring and reviewing our habits and self-imposed limits? Secondly, how skilful are we at learning about what is hidden, forgotten or unknown? And, thirdly, how do we communicate our know-how in a simple and understandable way?

No doubt these questions raise a number of tensions in human communication. Even with the best intentions and techniques of knowledge sharing, it is not foolproof. As soon as someone tries to communicate something they lose part of their message or insight. This can be seen when people try to write an idea down. It is very difficult to capture everything in a letter, email or a book. Even then, we have to expect that some of the material you share will be incorrect because it is based on inappropriate assumptions, context and facts. People need to constantly test and question their wisdom while also being prepared to explain the assumptions behind each story or message.

Getting our knowledge out is one thing, but then having it accepted or understood without modification is another. We need to follow up to ensure our communications are clear and acted upon. It is our innate ability to question knowledge at all levels that will ultimately determine whether we are able to transform an idea from something that may hold a silver lining to something golden.

In this regard it is important to understand the difference between what is called explicit and tacit knowledge. Explicit knowledge is know-how that can be written down. It normally takes the forms of checklists, formulas or procedures. Tacit knowledge, on the other hand, is wisdom or knowing that is locked in our mind or body. For example, if you asked me to tell you about where I live in Sydney, I could detail a number of facts about my suburb, but I would also tell you about my experiences. It is here in the stories of my experiences where you would move into my tacit knowledge. If you probed me you would discover more and more about the area in the city where I live and my own unique experience. It is here where you discover much deeper awareness than just facts. It is quite likely you could interview me for days and not touch the surface of what I know, not because I am especially smart but because in my mind are millions of stories and experiences. This tacit knowledge is priceless because it comes from direct experience.

Let us take the example of the Sydney Olympic Organising Committee for the 2000 Olympics Games. At the completion of the Atlanta Games in 1996, the Sydney committee decided to acquire many of the files from the running of the US games. On the surface, it seemed this pile of information was very useful, but much of it was not. Sure, many of the systems and procedures were similar, but the context was different and that made much of the transfer of know-how difficult. What helped more was the real-life visits of Sydney staff to Atlanta, recording videos and audiotapes, observing what was actually happening and attending an after-games debriefing.

As you would expect, tacit knowledge can take various forms. It could involve personal approaches to situations or problems including how decisions are made and in what order. It could detail deeper wisdom behind the routines, standard operating procedures and intellectual property. Tacit knowledge could be body and mind skills, which require practice to master—for example, how to lead a group discussion, to tile a bathroom or swim breaststroke. People can read about these skills but it is the practice and experience that grows their capability. Finally, there are mental models or schemes where people have developed a framework to make sense of a phenomenon or some hard-to-grasp situation—for example, how to manage hostile customers, or how to cope with stress. When you quiz someone about this level of tacit knowledge they could give you a list of possible frameworks, metaphors or theories to help them deal with the situation being discussed—all of which could be vitally important to a business or career.

The difficulty in extracting tacit knowledge is that much of it lies dormant in our minds, and is often left unspoken and unsaid. If you wish to reap the benefit of deeper tacit knowledge people need to become skilled at digging out this deeper know-how. Of course, some of this knowledge may be highly confidential, and so this issue would need to be discussed beforehand. However, by making an extra effort to record, observe and write down tacit knowledge, you can start to understand what and why people think the way they do.

There are numerous ways to help the sharing of tacit knowledge. Here are eleven examples:

1. Have people tell relevant stories, saying what they did and what they learnt.
2. When you are coaching, think aloud. Share what you are exploring and why.
3. Write down the history of an important experience. Then discuss the thinking and insight that came from each stage of your experience.
4. Write a case study based on a real-life situation. Then have a team of people explore their approaches to the situation.
5. Do plenty of reviews of what is actually occurring during an experience.
6. Encourage people to share their new understanding when they are experiencing new knowledge.

7. Use experts to develop models or frameworks from people's tacit experience.
8. Watch how others interpret and experiment with an idea. If you are the originator of the idea you could gain greater insight.
9. Take a theory or a hypothesis and test it. Take abstract notions and hunches and dig around and see what works or does not work.
10. Set up informal chats and dig deeper into what is on people's minds. Freewheeling conversations provide wonderful anecdotes and ways of thinking.
11. Organise Knowledge Fairs (see Chapter 5) to explore thinking, work in progress and test assumptions. The greater the cross-fertilisation and collaboration the better.

Finally, for the simpler, explicit knowledge ensure that the knowledge is properly codified and accessible to the right people. Having a large database of lessons learnt can be useful, but it must be well organised and easily retrievable. A large reservoir of stored knowledge is worthless unless it is put to use and is frequently updated and improved.

Summary

There are many ways a business can increase commitment to knowledge sharing. Firstly, the business planning process needs to bring people together from diverse backgrounds to discuss how change can be made to work. Secondly, sell the case for change by communicating stories and evidence that shows what behaviour is expected and what is possible. Here real-life people and testimonials work best. Thirdly, circulate knowledge by making it easy, safe and mutually beneficial. Finally, perfect the art of digging out deeper, tacit knowledge in a way that it has meaning and value to others in the business. Most of all we need to accept that even with the best intentions in the world, knowledge sharing is not a panacea—it is often subject to biases and bad conclusions. Always question and explore conclusions, assumptions and findings before assuming what you experience is correct.

CHAPTER 8

Riding the waves of change

'We are drowning in information and starving for knowledge.'—PHIL HARKINS, LOUIS CARTER AND AMY TIMMINS

Riding the waves of change requires:

- leadership that inspires confidence and hope
- auditing how well the business communicates
- growing knowledge-enhancing customers, suppliers and contractors
- linking business, individual and team thinking
- regular reviews of our knowledge assets.

Saving people from drowning

Like many people, I love to go to the beach. Whether swimming or watching from the shore, I often marvel at the temperament of the sea. Every minute seems like another episode of life. One second the sea can be calm and tranquil, and then without notice a large wave comes roaring towards the shore. If you are swimming you need to contend with these surges and changes around you by staying afloat, and by being relaxed and confident in the water.

Similarly, when it comes to winning the knowledge game we need to be ready for the next wave of change that comes our way. On a personal, team and business level we need to continually scan the horizon, being ready to respond to what is happening around us. At times, we may feel a little out of our depth and swamped by the next wave, but by remaining calm, hopeful and alert we will live to fight another day.

In the twenty-first century business, it is also easy to be drowned by information. We all have large volumes of information, directions and messages bombarding us. For example, the US Department of Commerce now estimates that the Internet is doubling in size every seventy days. The same growth is happening in business—for example, it is estimated that one of Xerox's computer databases currently holds more than 30 000 records of information. Research at Northrop Grumman has shown that even with the help of the Internet people are struggling to connect with the people they need to do their job (www.northropgrumman.com). Northrop Grumman estimates that on average knowledge workers can spend six weeks per year searching for experts to complete their work. IRN Services estimates that information professionals can spend up to 15 hours per week searching for information on the Internet, with only 44 per cent of their searches perceived as effective.

This evidence suggests that staying afloat in an information society is an immense challenge. It is interesting that even with elaborate search engines and the latest technology, people are struggling to stay informed and up-to-date. If any manager can help their people, customers and business partners handle these stresses they will love you for it. This translates into creating business systems that are clear, user friendly and supportive. Decision makers need to take every opportunity to assist people to regenerate and consolidate. This is particularly the case in tough times, when it is very easy to feel a little wounded, fragile and burnt out.

Just as when we are swimming in the ocean we need to help people stay afloat and enjoy the experience.

Removing the veil of secrecy

As discussed previously, businesses are not always a haven for winning the knowledge game. They are stuck in trying to second-guess what is happening. This is particularly the case when secrecy, hearsay and bullying are part of how a business operates.

To help overcome such difficulties we need to expose the behaviours that are causing damage. The more transparent and honest the conversation the more likely home truths will be discussed. This is not about running a propaganda campaign; it is about giving people meaningful feedback on what is the current state of play. This information needs to be placed in the hands of people who can suggest positive ways of proceeding.

When the plans and actions are decided managers need to back this up with a well-thought-out communications strategy. Choosing what to communicate is never easy; but from experience the answer is most likely *more* often rather than *less* often. Lend Lease Corporation is one global business that works hard to share information about the state of the business and to inform people what is happening. Like many organisations it publishes company news each day on its website. The goal is not to drown people in information but to feed them mission-critical knowledge. Similarly, government organisations such as the Australian Bureau of Statistics have daily updates of corporate and team news.

Whatever your business size or type, make it your job to audit the quality of your communications process on a regular basis—whether it is hit rates on a new web page or feedback from people about what they have learnt from a staff meeting. Communication audits can take various forms, ranging from conducting formal surveys of people's perceptions to vetting whether the key corporate messages are known and understood.

Here again the role of managers and team leaders is vitally important. If they do their job properly the business will work so much better.

Remember to be very clever in how your business grabs and holds people's attention. In this 15-minute world it is very easy to become sidetracked.

Additionally it is worth noting that larger to medium-sized businesses are increasingly appointing communications managers to keep an eye on the flow and quality of knowledge. Such appointments can improve the quality of communication and assist decision making.

Sponsoring connection and interactivity

Most best practice businesses pride themselves on the interaction between their employees, customers, suppliers and, increasingly, their competitors. The result is higher levels of know-how and stronger business performance. Business-to-business (B2B) e-commerce is a modern-day example of how a close connection and better interaction is leading to improved competitive advantage. McKinsey and Company estimates that B2B transactions will be worth over US$1.4 trillion worldwide in 2003, with the Asia Pacific accounting for 20 per cent of this figure (see www.mckinseyquarterly.com). The research group Jupiter Media Metix estimates that, by 2005, this figure will have grown to US$6.3 trillion, where 42 per cent of total sales will be done over the Internet (see www.jupiterresearch.com). So apart from the benefits of exchanging knowledge, there is staggering growth in business transactions such as tendering and ordering both products and services.

The growth in Internet-generated B2B e-commerce is based on the economies of scale that come from seamless transactions between suppliers and businesses. Simple examples could include expanding your expertise in the marketplace by sharing know-how, getting faster and cheaper services such as a printing job or buying a new version of software. Business has certainly moved a long way from just ringing a contact from the local telephone directory or relying on just one trusted referral. To be competitive in today's workplace an Internet presence has become essential.

As you would expect the types of Internet-enabled B2B alliances are quite diverse and are in a constant state of flux. The key players change on a daily basis. However, there are a number of broad categories worth exploring, beginning with businesses that help suppliers and buyers to find each other, such as eBay. Then you move to other types, such as Amazon who are a clearinghouse for goods and services. There is Expertcentral, which assists people to share ideas or ask experts for opinions. Businesses such as Cisco Systems connect customers, partners, suppliers and employees in a global supply network by giving immediate access to supply and demand information in a host of areas including manufacturing, finance and design. FedEx helps people to get the latest information on delivery and distribution. If you are an architect, contractor or professional and wish to share documents and conversations on such issues as large construction projects Buzzsaw can help. No doubt in the years ahead this avenue of assistance and service delivery will expand into many more categories and features.

Of course connection and interactivity is not just business to business, it can also include employee to employee and business to customer. The size and scale of the Internet gives potential access to millions of possible contacts and opportunities. Depending on your interests, anyone can join a discussion group, join a chat room, send email or connect with someone new. People no longer have to wait to get an answer; we all have an opportunity to be free agents for our learning.

However, with this access comes the responsibility to ensure we are not abusing the privilege. When seeking our answers and exploring new pathways of knowledge, integrity and ethics are very important. For example, not overstaying our welcome, dumping people with junk and unsolicited advertising or deploying careless language can quickly destroy potentially worthwhile e-relationships. A little respect and graciousness can go a long way.

Finally, it is worth noting that Internet-enhanced business-to-customer (B2C) relationships will be explored in more depth in Chapter 12 on 'Increasing customer loyalty'. For now it is important to introduce the concept of building a customer relationship based on greater openness and learning. I know from my consulting business that close relationships are the most important ingredient of success. Without close and intimate sharing of knowledge I would never grow and develop. In many ways business success is directly linked to how knowledge-enhancing contacts are obtained, nurtured and maintained over time. In business this notion can be extended to business interfaces with other parties, whether they are suppliers, contractors or business partners—while not forgetting the wonderful value of knowledge-enhancing employees as well.

Opening up networks and shared advantage

In modern business there needs to be a strong link between individual effort, teamwork and organisational objectives. The more aligned this relationship, the better the chance for ongoing excellence and innovation. A range of people management strategies can be used to keep the best talent, including careful recruitment, good training and regular career development discussions. Such strategies will help create fertile ground for opening up networks, the flow of knowledge and shared advantage—all of which are essential for stimulating a work attitude that generates competitive advantage.

There are a number of ways to open up networks and share the advantage of knowledge. Here are five of my favourites:

1. Be spontaneous, tell stories over breakfast, lunch or a coffee; but do it in a relaxed and friendly way. If you have a tearoom, spend a little money on paint and decorations to give it an informal and inclusive atmosphere. I even know a manager who invested in a mini-fridge in the office so that people would come in and chat over a cold drink. What a stroke of genius, and most importantly it worked.

2. Have people brainstorm their ideas on what could be done to free up the level of sharing and exchange. Ask for feedback on the following questions: How can we better transfer what we know or need to know? How can we make knowledge more accessible and more interesting to people? How could we better grab attention and involvement? Which methods and systems are currently in use? How can we use these better? Which practices, rules and behaviours kill off innovation and the flow of knowledge? Where should we start? And how will we review progress?

3. Create simple ways for people to input their discoveries and questions. Having peers working on the material together and having third parties review it can often assist this. Decide which knowledge is easily recorded and written down (i.e. checklists and quick tips) and which is more tacit or complex in nature.

4. Open up access to the Internet and encourage people to apply what they learn from their discoveries and feed it back into the business. Create home pages that connect people and their wisdom.

Place communities of practice, mentors and knowledge archives up front on the home page. Reduce the emphasis on information and increase the emphasis on knowledge. Where possible have people meet face to face or use technologies such as video-conferencing and telephone conferencing, webcam and file-sharing software to stimulate collaboration. Assist the cause by providing a series of incentives. British Telecom have in the past given a monthly reward for knowledge sharing, including small monetary rewards to the most prolific provider of valuable knowledge on their intranet. Another reward was for the person who answered the most queries in the 'ask me another' folder on the business home page; and another was given to the person who provided the most valuable piece of knowledge.

5. Encourage people to be actively involved in organising and presenting knowledge-sharing events. These can range from simple and inexpensive gatherings over sandwiches and soft drinks to major extravaganzas involving holiday resorts or hotel venues. Remember expense is not the barometer of success; it is the creativity, stimulation and mutual support that comes from such gatherings that is far more important.

We can never fully anticipate what will happen when we ask people to interact and share knowledge. It is imperative that any potential conflicts that may occur are anticipated. Be sure to set workable expectations from the start, although you do not want people to be paralysed by them. All the emails, websites and conversations need to lead to something tangible and worthwhile. Somewhere along the line someone needs to take a stand and summarise what is being learnt and give feedback on what is not working.

For example, in project teams people can be so nice and polite that they struggle to make headway. Or a team leader can easily create a nightmare democracy where people are so consultation crazy that nothing ever eventuates. At the other extreme a process can quickly suffer from a loss of interest and motivation where a specific outcome is driven too hard by one, or two, key people. Again there are no simple answers. It is easy to take the middle ground, but at times such a position may not be right. You just need to read the situation and play the game as you see it.

Throwing out 'use-by-date' knowledge

One of the greatest benefits of knowledge work and sharing wisdom is that we uncover what has served its 'use-by date'. Of course there are times when learnt wisdom may make a comeback, but most of the time it will not. Discarding non-critical knowledge assets is an important part of the improvement cycle, as it frees up a business for different thinking, savings and better resource management. For example, each year I take what many people would say is a radical step. I venture into my office with empty boxes and then throw out 20 per cent of my books and about 40 per cent of my accumulated paperwork and information from my computer databases. My books are donated to my local library and the paperwork is recycled. In doing so I feel I have cleared my mind of clutter and created the opportunity for something new. Of course, vital pieces of knowledge are still safely kept or archived, but as a result of this throwing-out process I feel infinitely better prepared for the next wave of change.

In a larger business throwing out use-by-date knowledge is also very important. Throwing out assets may involve selling or licensing intellectual property, not renewing a patent, outsourcing a business function to another provider, terminating an old system or even changing staff. If the right decision is made, new relationships, better systems and a stronger competitive strategy will unfold. If you remove or outsource knowledge assets for the wrong reason your actions can come back to haunt you—so tread carefully. Avoid the slash and burn approach. The wrong cost-cutting exercise can quickly leave you with a vacuum of talent to run the business.

There are of course many thousands of businesses shedding knowledge assets each week. For example, Sara Lee discarded much of its sales force to concentrate more on marketing, sales and new product development by using B2C e-commerce. Ericsson outsourced its entire production of mobile telephones and concentrated more of its efforts on quality assurance. As you would expect these types of decisions are often very painful or difficult. Such decisions often involve other competing considerations such as social responsibility or losing unprofitable customers and protecting the future of employees.

Finally, instead of jumping in straight away and buying new systems or acquiring new knowledge you may wish to put your toe in the water first and then explore possibilities without unnecessary risks. Three common strategies include:

1. pooling resources and doing research before committing to major change
2. forming a joint venture with a business partner where outlays and risks can be shared
3. conducting tests of a product or service in the marketplace before proceeding.

Summary

Riding the waves of change requires a diversity of leadership, technology and business skills. Business needs to help people stay afloat and gain control by providing practical support to build their capability and zest for learning. New networks and knowledge-enhancing relationships need to be identified and built to grow competitive advantage. Individual and team creativity must be integrated and blended into the business brain by involving people in important decision-making and knowledge-sharing activities. Finally, important decisions are required to audit existing knowledge and to cast off assets that are no longer required.

CHAPTER 9

Sustaining and keeping talent

'People do not leave bad companies, they leave bad bosses.'—Dr Beverly Kaye

Sustaining and keeping talent requires:

- going beyond money as the sole motivator
- concentrating on both individual and team retention
- avoiding the stereotyping of people
- discussing what personal success really means
- being creative in how you say thankyou.

Discovering passions and dreams

There is little point investing countless hours trying to win the knowledge game if you are unable to attract and keep the talent you need for your business. Each business needs to find the right formula to ensure their people are willing, skilled and motivated. People must feel that their work provides a pathway to a better life and hope for the future. To inspire and keep talent we must assist people to extract meaning out of what they are doing so that they can progress, build confidence and grow. Most of all a business must foster a culture or attitude that rewards the flow of ideas so that a better future can be generated for everyone's benefit.

To do this requires a unique chemistry—one that is fuelled by mutual respect and an emotional bond between people. Only then do we have the capacity to drive the collaboration and know-how needed to achieve better results. As a 2002 study by Hewitt Associates and the Australian Graduate School of Management found, the best employers excel in four areas (see http://was.hewitt.com/hewitt):

1. people leadership
2. accelerated learning and development
3. compelling employment offers that provide a higher purpose and a different work experience
4. a business culture driven by performance, results, fun, celebration and recognition.

As one explores the advice on keeping and inspiring talent it is very easy to be smothered by a multitude of options, programs and strategies. Recent writing has been prolific and it is easy to become confused. However, some simple things can make a world of difference. Most of all people must feel that they can help to improve things and make a positive contribution. So there must always be abundant opportunities for people to share and listen to each other's passions, dreams and plans. When this occurs as the norm rather than the exception a business can dramatically improve its chances of going beyond the attraction of money as the sole motivator and discover the real motivation of its people. Instead of jumping to a salary increase as a solution look for other factors. These could include building a friendlier workplace, regular meetings, good induction programs, fairness and equal employment opportunity, shared spaces such as tearooms, organised social activities, working in teams, training courses, formal networking opportunities such as employee interest groups, sporting or other clubs and, finally, communities of practice.

A colleague of mine, Susie Linder-Pelz, said to me a decade ago that we should be less interested in absentee-ism and more interested in presentee-ism. In other words, looking at who turns up to work is only a small part of the equation; managers need to stimulate higher levels of contribution and enthusiasm from those who contribute to the business every day. Be prepared to look at the root causes of poor performance and encourage people to get more meaning in what they do. Be prepared to listen to the whole message—however pleasant or unpleasant it might be. Each manager or team leader must see their responsibility as one that involves the capability of fostering and nurturing talent. If we do not have the skill or will to do this we will have a huge impasse in the system.

During the last decade, research by organisations such as the University of Michigan and websites such as www.keepem.com has consistently shown that you can entice people with money and perks, but you will not be able to keep them if they become unhappy, unmotivated or undervalued. This is particularly the case for the more mobile, younger and free-spirited individual who knows where their opportunities lie and where they can go.

Alternatively, a very low turnover may not always be wonderful news. It may mean a business full of people who just want to turn up to work even though they may feel deeply unhappy, alienated and powerless. This is bad news for performance and innovation. Business needs to build high value and foster high-loyalty relationships where both the individual and the business benefits. We hardly want people just serving time. As John Herbert, the former CEO of the Australian Institute of Management, Queensland Branch, says, 'people may say they have had ten years' experience but in fact it is ten times one year's experience'.

The Saratoga Institute also says that between 50 and 80 per cent of workers' satisfaction is directly related to their relationship with their boss (Fitz-enz, 2000; www.keepem.com). If they have a healthy and open relationship they will most likely stay. In studies of over 70 000 exit interviews, the institute has found that the main reason a person voluntarily leaves is the behaviour of their supervisor. The second reason is perceived lack of growth opportunities. So having a bad boss is not good news for keeping talent or what some people call human capital. Wide-ranging research also supports the view that meaningful and challenging work, a chance to learn and grow, fair compensation, a good work environment, and recognition and respect are particularly important reasons to stay in a job.

A study of the Australian retail sector published by the Work and Family Unit in the Australian Department of Employment and Workplace Relations puts a different spin on the talent challenge. They discovered that retail employees seek much more control over working hours. This is not surprising, given the length of trading hours in most retail outlets these days. Higher pay and better career opportunities were also a point of contention for most retail employees. Part-time employees were found to be just as committed to business success as full-time workers, and the study found that many retail workers want a career and are becoming more and more careful about shopping around to find a good employer. As Dr Boxall from the Australian Retailers Association says, 'people want to work in an organisation that values their contribution and assists them to achieve a work–home balance. The needs of business are changing too, and there is opportunity here for win–win situations.'

In the nursing profession there has been a host of recent studies that indicate that the high turnover of nurses and the failure to attract new people to the profession is largely driven by a lack of faith that nurses can change the health system. There are also concerns over work–life balance and the limited time available for spending with their patients. Such issues will need to be addressed if the current trend of severe shortages is to be reversed.

It is clear that to sustain and keep talent we need outstanding people management. We need managers who demonstrate talent management as a core skill and motivation. We need people who are not caught up in their own self-importance, but are more interested in building the capabilities of people around them. We also need to develop a business culture where people constantly ask courageous questions of each other. For example: What would it take for you to stay? Or, alternatively, What might it take to lure you away? Such questions not only help uncover possible concerns and motivations but also show a genuine desire to help out and listen. This is vitally important for inspiring greater contribution and reducing the likelihood of people jumping ship or beginning a stream of departures.

The seven 'Sleeping Giants' of career management

To understand the changing face of talent management in modern business it is imperative to clearly understand and respect the seven 'Sleeping Giants' of career management. These are:

1. the haunting cost of turnover
2. a chronic skills shortage
3. higher career mobility
4. the Pied Piper effect
5. the 'working poor'
6. a craving for balance
7. a boom of depression.

The haunting cost of turnover

Beverley Kaye and Sharon Jordan-Evans (1999) in their book *Love 'Em or Lose 'Em* say that the cost of replacing people can be between 70 and 200 per cent of a person's annual salary. Technology workers, professionals and managers cost twice as much as other employees to replace. These estimates are not surprising, particularly when the costs are tallied up. Costs can include:

* recruitment and advertising
* travel and accommodation
* downtime while people conduct interviews and make decisions
* extra workload pressures on remaining staff
* hiring temporary staff
* downtime in productivity as the new person or team learns the ropes.

Then there is the loss of knowledge, connections and networks that comes with the departure of vital people. There are also hidden intangible costs such as reduced reputation, loss of customers and brain drain. To make matters worse a former staff member can start producing wonderful results elsewhere, which can create all sorts of consequences in a competitive marketplace.

The reality of turnover is that all the intellectual property and know-how in the world will not make a scrap of difference if you do not have a sound talent-retention strategy. This is particularly relevant in gloomy economic and employment cycles when people may not choose to jump ship. Instead they may opt for greater sick leave rather than depart, resulting in another form of loss to the business.

A chronic skills shortage

According to the US Census Bureau, sixty-one countries are unable to find the skilled people they need to perform the jobs they require. In recent years this has been very noticeable in professions such as information technology, management, teaching and, as already mentioned, nursing. Two main factors contribute to this shortfall—firstly, the rapid pace of change and, secondly, the low numbers of people in the age group of 25 to 44 years of age. The implication is that finding and keeping talent is far more difficult now than it was in the past.

Further evidence can be drawn from the following trends in developed economies:

* A study by Accenture found that retaining the best talent was the biggest people-management challenge, with 57 per cent of organisations surveyed noting this as critical (www.business2.com; article by Tess Romia, June 2001). Another study by McKinsey and Company found that in 75 per cent of organisations, the senior managers did not believe they had the talent to perform their current responsibilities (www.mckinsey.de, April 2001).
* The American Society for Training and Development—in 2000 in a keynote address at its annual conference—estimated that 74 per cent of the US workforce will need to be retrained by 2010. Likewise, a study by TMP/Hudson Global Resources in Australia of 500 senior executives found that 76 per cent of businesses required upskilling to work effectively, while up to 66 per cent had a limited understanding or commitment to the values of the organisation (au.tmp.com).

- US managerial jobs will increase by 25 per cent in the next 15 years, but the availability of 25–44 year olds is expected to decline by 15 per cent (www.keepem.com).
- It is expected that in the next ten years, one-third of nurses in Australia will leave the workforce. This shortage is also being experienced in many other countries such as the US and the UK. One major factor is the ageing workforce, with the average age of a nurse being around 45 years.
- The shortage of talent is being fuelled in countries where there is a lower workforce participation rate of 55–64 year olds. For example, in the US the participation rate in this age bracket is 60 per cent as against 49 per cent in Australia (Needham, 2002).
- A Development Dimensions International (DDI) survey showed that 91 per cent of Australian organisations had difficulty finding talent at all levels, particularly at senior levels (www.shlgroup.com/au/news/2002/leadership.shtm).

Higher career mobility

During the last decade there has been a noticeable change from full-time employment to part-time, contract or on-call workforces. We see this across all industries, including manufacturing, retail and aviation. In the US 26 per cent of the current workforce is temporary, part-time or contingent, and this is expected to rise to 41 per cent by 2010, with even higher rates in places like Sweden and Norway. In Australia just under 25 per cent of the workforce is part-time. Interestingly there is a larger percentage of part-time workers who would like more work. This so-called underemployed segment of part-time workers has risen 24 per cent in the last two years. This is particularly relevant to the over-45-year-old bracket.

The trend to greater casualisation of the workforce is also indicative of individuals seeking greater freedom, balance and leverage of their time, resulting in them having a number of employers. At the same time employers are seeking to keep costs down by maintaining a smaller and leaner operation. As a result a host of strategies is being employed to import know-how by other means, whether hiring more contract staff, employment of experts, acquiring consultants or changing work practices to be more flexible.

One of the consequences of mobility is the increasing difficulty in building and sustaining a unified business identity, particularly when a workforce is in constant transition. In many cases the majority of people who worked in a business three years ago no longer work in that business today. This is particularly the case in the more qualified or high-demand jobs. Creative strategies need to be deployed to help the right talent to stay and contribute longer by giving greater opportunities to grow. For businesses such as management consulting firms, this may mean having an abundance of high quality resources, tools and expert networks for staff to use. Employees are then less interested in leaving because they are attached to the high quality of knowledge available in the business.

Similarly special care must be taken to nurture and support staff who often take up new or extra responsibility when staffing levels are low. This is particularly the case in shift work or in high-pressure work. Left unattended, people can quickly experience a fear of responsibility, or of becoming ineffective if left unchecked.

The consequence of higher career mobility means a business must ensure people are looked after and the best people are retained. To be successful, business leaders must increasingly see employment and hiring as a win–win partnership rather than a boss–subordinate relationship. We can no longer see employees as people who come to work for us. It is better to reverse the mindset to ask how can a business inspire higher levels of contribution and commitment. As notable management guru Peter Drucker said, we need to treat people as volunteers, not conscripts. As a result businesses are increasingly exploring new and different incentive programs such as paying for contribution rather than hours of attendance. Of course a sound approach to the protection of intellectual property is also needed. This is discussed in the next chapter.

The Pied Piper effect

Job-hopping is now the nature of the beast in many industries. If you get someone to stay and contribute in a job for eighteen months you are doing well. Research by the Saratoga Institute indicates that after about two years of service you will normally experience some difficulties keeping people unless you have taken corrective action (Kaye and

Jordon-Evans, 1999). An individual entering the workforce for the first time is now likely to have on average nine job changes by the time they turn thirty-two years of age. A 2001 study of 1759 people on monster.com.au discovered that 90 per cent of those surveyed expected to have a career change in the next five years.

As already indicated, loyalty is often at its highest at team level and not at a business-enterprise level. The consequence of this is that individuals will often stick together, even at the expense of the organisation.

For many businesses, getting too close to staff and building a shared commitment is seen as just too hard. This is particularly the case where managers are too preoccupied on matters other than people development and as a result see their staff and know-how as a dispensable resource that can be hired and fired at a moment's notice. This common situation was vividly highlighted by a recent study of six hundred CEOs and one thousand middle to senior managers. The study found that most CEOs expected about 10 per cent of their managers to leave the company over the coming six to twelve months, while more than 50 per cent of managers surveyed indicated they intended to leave (Moullakis, 2003).

An interesting side product of team loyalty is that turnover is not just an individual issue; it has become a team or tribal issue. Like in the famous children's story of the *Pied Piper of Hamelin*, whole teams can often get up and leave or are headhunted en masse to move to another business in what is often called the Pied Piper effect. The result of such a loss of team talent can be catastrophic. Businesses are responding to the Pied Piper effect with a long list of strategies. Such strategies range from sophisticated retention programs to simple ideas like that used by some Silicon Valley organisations, whereby employers are sending past employees postcards with the theme 'Is the grass greener?' to try and entice them back. In some cases people discover that the imagery given in recruitment by a new employer is not matched by reality and return in either a full-time, part-time or contract capacity.

The 'working poor'

One of the more disturbing trends of modern workplaces is the increased incidence of the 'working poor'. The working poor can be defined as those people who, even though working, are unable to stay above the poverty line. Not surprisingly, many people in low-wage jobs do not have the education level or accreditation to get better-paid jobs. The National Coalition against Poverty in Australia and global organisations such as the International Labor Organization and UNICEF have been drawing attention to the issues of the working poor as well as child labour, educational opportunities, Internet access and unethical business practices in an attempt to improve the situation.

There is a host of statistics and stories to support the conclusion of a widening gap between the haves and the have-nots. Further, there is ongoing community disquiet over the ever-increasing level of senior executive salaries. Businesses need to be sensitive to these problems and be prepared to balance economics and share price with issues of fairness, equity and employee loyalty. Just because someone is employed does not necessarily mean that they are able to sustain the quality of life they need for themselves and their family. For example, Japan has a relatively low unemployment rate compared to Spain, but both countries have child poverty rates of 12 per cent.

A craving for balance

Many people are currently reviewing their lives and searching for new ways to find greater balance and do what they love. We see this increasingly, where people are choosing different lifestyles or employment options. This trend is set to continue, particularly as cyberspace becomes more accessible. As Dr Boxall from the Australian Retailers Association says, people want to work in organisations that value their contribution and assist them to achieve a work–home balance. In recent years Australian organisations that have excelled in work–family policy and practice are IBM Australia, the Australian Catholic University, the Australian Film Commission, SC Johnson, Sisters Inside Inc., Somerville Community Services Inc., Yarra Valley Water, Paul Shelley Electrical, the Australian Health Management Group and the Commonwealth Department of Family and Community Services.

A study commissioned by the Australian Council of Trade Unions provides extra evidence to a world trend that people are craving balance in their lives (Horin and Wilson, 2001). It found that one in five Australian workers now works more than 50 hours per week.

The study found that long and unreasonable working hours were damaging families, friendships and community life. It is common for some people to go for days without seeing their children and partners, and missing out on key milestones in their lives such as birthdays and anniversaries. Understaffing and/or talent shortages have meant countless emails and mobile telephone messages invading people's private time. Workers who elect to spend more time with their families are viewed with suspicion.

Younger people are also highly susceptible to hitting the wall of burnout at an earlier age if not well looked after. I know from personal observation I am increasingly seeing 25-year-olds washed up and opting to escape from work to recharge or start a new lifestyle. We only have to visit many call centres and telemarketing businesses to see ample proof of early-age burnout. This is not surprising given the ever-increasing pressure of people to do more with less, resulting in a waning of people's health and lack of work–life balance.

A boom of depression

Studies by such organisations as the Australian Medical Association and the St Vincent de Paul Society provide solid evidence that human depression is fast becoming one of the biggest health issues facing developed economies. It is predicted that in Australia depression will be the second biggest health concern by 2020 (*The Medical Journal of Australia*, 2001). By 2020, one in three people in Australia will be experiencing depression or will be on medication. It is also estimated that of the 90 per cent of people who see a general practitioner once a year, 49 per cent showed evidence of common mental disorders. While 20 per cent of Australians are reported to have at least one mental disorder, the figure for the homeless is 75 per cent. These observations are supported by similar studies by the World Bank and World Health Organization. They report that mental illness now constitutes one of the largest causes of disability for Western communities.

The implications of this last Sleeping Giant are profound. It translates into a vivid realisation that managing stress and associated depression is now a major priority in sustaining and keeping talent. Concentrating solely on ideas and innovation is not enough. We must focus on people's mental health, well-being and relationships to ensure depression and anxiety are not left unchecked. Business leaders must foster a culture that helps people to cope and self-manage without unnecessary levels of stress and depression. Studies across the world have consistently shown a very strong correlation between stress, lost productivity and excessive working hours.

As Professor Robert Lane from Yale University says, 'the most powerful cause of depression is not brain derailment but disruption of family and friendly relations. Friendship (the main contributor to happiness) is not a market commodity.' So if you want to help reduce depression and improve talent levels, take an interest in people, and make them feel special, valued and part of a team.

Other findings on emotional health include:

- British academic Bill Lucas says, 'the brain's efficiency can be reduced by up to 90 per cent while working under pressure'. Emotions, and our ability to cope with pressure, have a massive impact on our ability to think, problem solve and communicate, whether we are conscious of it or not.
- People who are unable to effectively manage their stress have a 40 per cent higher death rate than more emotionally managed individuals (Eysenck, 1988).
- Bryan Stock, an authority on 'emotional intelligence', says that one emotion can lead to 1300 chemical reactions in the body.
- The HeartMath research centre at www.heartmath.com has shown that spending just five minutes of feeling genuine appreciation for the things in our lives that we value can boost our immune system for up to six hours.

Building capability

It is obvious that sustaining and keeping talent needs a plan of action as one responds in a confident way to any of the seven Sleeping Giants of career management that your business might be facing. If key people leave unannounced, taking with them years of know-how and expertise, we have a problem and it must be fixed. Thinking how we could have managed a person better after they have left is far too late. We must inspire and motivate people while we are with them. Our leadership and management is vitally important.

Of course wasted talent is not just about unplanned departures: it also involves a careful strategy of downsizing and retrenchment. With a little more planning we can save significant embarrassment. Workplaces are full of people who have been hired back at far more expensive rates to solve issues.

So what can one do to build the capability to keep and sustain talent? Of course simple respect and better people management is a great start. Four principles are central to this cause. Firstly, the business needs to inspire a vision and a compelling case for people to stay. Secondly, we need to help people gain a greater sense of control and choice in what they are doing. Thirdly, good people need special care; just because they are performing well does not mean everything is OK. Finally, there needs to be effort to identify career goals that stimulate motivation and learning. When this starts to occur, the chances of sustaining and keeping people will be so much higher.

However, we cannot assume that managers and team leaders have these skills. From experience, it seems such basic people management skills are rare in many businesses. People need reminders and training to help fill this gap. The business should clearly explain the importance and consequences of better talent management. For example, most people would agree that growing competitive advantage is impossible if there is extraordinarily high turnover, or if people hate working with their manager. It is particularly important that people's performance is reviewed honestly. Steering clear of stereotyping based on age, gender, race, disability and educational background is a great start. For example common assumptions need to be questioned. Do all young males really have potential? Does a young female really need time to grow? Tread very carefully.

To help sustain and keep talent in your business, listed below are fifty talent-building ideas.

Fifty talent-building ideas

Sharpening your public image

1. Before looking for new talent, make sure you know what skills and capabilities you are seeking.

2. Share stories of your successes and how you treat your staff. Testimonials and case studies are very useful in the marketplace. If you have won awards, or you are seen as best practice, let people know.

3. Make sure your public documentation is available via the Internet or in paper form and looks professional.

4. Attend trade shows and share your story. Do public presentations and press releases about what you do. A little self-promotion can work wonders.

5. Join industry networks, professional associations and voluntary organisations, and be a good corporate citizen. Learn who are the best at sustaining and keeping talent and discover their lessons.

6. Form close relationships with universities, schools and trade colleges. Get a good name with potential hirers. Being a good corporate citizen also works wonders.

Recruitment

7. Seriously consider recruitment training. Discover how biases, unfairness, discrimination and poor interviewing and screening can hurt you.

8. Advertise vacancies in multiple sites and locations. Make sure you are not neglecting your own staff before looking elsewhere. Set up a job posting for internal job application processing.

9. Join forces with other businesses to form an industry response to the shortage of talent, detailing available career and training opportunities.

10. Consider the advantages and disadvantages of securing the services of a recruitment firm or employment agency. Agree on a monitoring and review process.

11. If it is appropriate, explore talent from overseas or another geographic region or industry. Engage services with professionals who work from remote locations and consider using technology such as file sharing, email and threaded discussion groups.

12. Make sure you honestly communicate career paths and opportunities. Do not oversell the job and be candid, realistic and honest.

13. When people join you, welcome them as full members of the team, in whatever capacity they are filling. It does not matter if they are temporary staff, full-time, part-time or a contractor, they must be valued and recognised.

14. Make sure employment contracts and confidentiality agreements are fair and reasonable and that both parties agree.

15. After hiring is complete, conduct post-interview discussions with both successful and unsuccessful applicants.

Day-to-day support

16. Make sure people have the right tools, contacts and information to do their jobs. An induction package is a good idea.

17. Make sure you discuss planned business changes. Frequently ask people for their ideas and ask how they believe they can contribute more.

18. Inspire loyalty and provide continual feedback with both integrity and honesty.

19. Provide regular career coaching and planning advice. In some cases, consider probation or job trials to see how people fit into different roles.

20. Create meaningful ways to celebrate successes and recognise contribution. Build a sense of community, team spirit and belonging.

21. Ensure good professional and emotional support is available.

22. Hold performance discussions to ensure adequate and relevant feedback. Again training and user-friendly assistance is vital.

23. Make sure you are looking after the people who are staying.

24. Find creative ways to say thankyou, and have fun.

Learning and development

25. Use mentors and coaches to develop potential.

26. Make sure the job is seen as the real classroom. Undertake knowledge sharing to the maximum.

27. Invest in in-house training; consider both face-to-face and e-learning.

28. Use public courses and hire expert educators and consultants if you need to train a team.

29. Reward learning and provide incentives for people to share their wisdom.
30. Make sure you capture vital knowledge. Place critical knowledge on business archives and Help Desks.
31. Make sure people get feedback on their leadership. Consider a range of self-help tools for ongoing development in how to sustain and keep talent. Working smarter tools, such as business planning, time management and people management, are normally a great start.
32. Sponsor and encourage external study.
33. Encourage the establishment of informal learning through networks and community practice.

Job design

34. Ensure you have a succession plan. Consider future business strategies and your current talent. Chart the way forward—together.
35. Make sure performance goals are clear and understood. Discuss how work can be changed to provide greater stimulation and variety. Ask team members what would keep them in your team or what would encourage them to leave.
36. Hold managers and team leaders responsible for deploying sound retention and talent-nurturing practices. Move managers or team leaders who are causing you damage.
37. Use temporary projects and special assignments to build skills.
38. Reward the coaches and knowledge sharers.
39. Use job rotation to transfer people around—to spread and develop their capabilities and know-how.
40. Use your mentors, coaches and subject-matter experts as facilitators to help address chronic gaps in know-how in the business. Help people to position their knowledge for the future.
41. Use joint ventures with other organisations to build expertise and know-how.

Flexible work practices

42. Address work and family issues upfront, giving people the opportunity to discuss rosters, schedules, start and finish times, and holiday leave.

43. Deploy flexible work practices, such as part-time work, working from home, job sharing and reasonable working hours.
44. Use older workers and early retirees in a part-time or even full-time capacity. Provide a good mix of salary and options with flexible hours to suit their lifestyle.
45. Creatively use digital technology to engage talent—for example, telecommuting and virtual teams.

Protecting capability

46. When you hire special help, make sure some of their capabilities and know-how is captured and stays in the business.
47. Make sure you have agreed standards for protecting intellectual property.
48. When people leave make sure you hold exit interviews. Explore the reasons for departure, and extract ideas on making the business a better place to work.
49. If people leave, keep the relationship going and be a good citizen. Be gracious and noble because one day they may want to return or put in a good word for you. Allow them to retreat with dignity and grace.
50. Get an independent assessment of how your business performs in the area of sustaining and keeping talent.

Being a great employer

As one explores the terrain of talent management it is obvious that people management is a major influencing factor. In most cases, it is firmly in your control. Whatever the economic situation or business climate, efforts should be taken to keep a close eye on how people are feeling and performing. People need to know that they can feel empowered with the authority to do their job, while also recognising that what they are doing is adding something of value to society rather than just creating wealth or saving costs.

The best employers also take an active role in career planning. This often means jointly discussing what success means. For example, does someone really want a promotion? Or are they interested in other options like job stimulation, greater work–home balance or different levels of responsibility? Often helping someone to discover new career options can open up whole new avenues for adding value and learning more.

Let us say a person wants to be a journalist and their current job does not call on that skill. However, with a little creativity and task swapping this person could soon be performing more writing in their job, which could make a world of difference to their motivation and contribution to the business. Further, taking the writing responsibilities away from someone else may free them up to do something that they would prefer to be doing. In most cases people love you for being a little more receptive and flexible in how jobs and work are organised.

Good employers also see diversity as a plus. They engage talent by mixing and blending people from different backgrounds, whether it is different ages, expertise or cultures. This provides the creative tension needed for winning the knowledge game. For example, a young workforce may benefit from having older workers in the team, particularly if the benefit of having a greater pool of expertise is understood.

Finally, you may find it useful to do some reading on the specific needs of different age groups—for example, Baby Boomers, Generation X and Generation Y. People born in the 1960s to the mid-1970s (i.e. Generation X) are perceived to have quite different work expectations to Baby Boomers. However, we need to be careful in making generalisations. Although such reading could lead to a host of new ideas, be prepared to sit down and discuss unique needs face to face with the person concerned. Do not run off and buy a box full of baseball caps, order pizza or let people bring their pet to work if they think the idea is silly or just window dressing.

We cannot guess and make assumptions about people's needs. Listen to them and if appropriate conduct an independent survey to get a more accurate view of the talent picture and story.

Creating fun and rewards

Work can and should be fun. Enjoyable places of work can be entertaining and can give great comical relief as well as achieving visible results and outcomes. Work can supply a real sense of friendship, family and community, if we get the dynamics right. From my experience, the teams that show greatest creativity in how they say thankyou generate higher levels of commitment. So say yes to fun and rewards and help foster motivation, desire and contribution.

FedEx, for example, name their aeroplanes after the names of employees' children. Each time the company buys a new plane, employees are invited to submit their children's names and one is picked randomly. This is not an expensive exercise but it means so much to its workers. Such novelty is essential, as it helps to create a new and curious environment for learning.

Most of all business needs to loosen up, be less serious and grab every opportunity to build a positive attitude while doing a professional job. In saying this, you do not have to be a comedian and tell jokes every day, but it does help if you can find something to smile about on a regular basis. Whether it is having birthday cakes, bringing in baby photographs, or having a game of softball, look to have fun for yourself and your business.

Of course, these ideas have a non-monetary reward attached to them. They make people feel included, valued and important. Even a creative idea can become boring if it is overused. For example, some people are hooked on after-work drinks. Certainly these social functions can be a lot of fun but they can also be boring if they are poorly organised or overused. Why not spark your imagination and come up with some new ideas? Here are a few ideas I have observed that can help spark incentive:

- Let people change their working hours or duties.
- Purchase a theatre ticket or send a personal thankyou card.
- Acquire an award trophy or mention people's work in a report or newsletter.
- Invite someone to an important meeting.
- Pay for someone to attend a special conference or training course.
- Let someone have a car spot for a month.
- Give a small on-the-spot cash reward.

Summary

Sustaining and keeping talent is one of the biggest challenges in business. The solution lies in a variety of actions. First of all we need outstanding and effective leadership. Secondly, we need to discuss what people's dreams and passions are, and help them to map out a career plan. Thirdly, business must adapt and work with the challenges of chronic skill shortages and the lack of balance in people's lives to give them the best chance of performing in a lasting way. The best employers move beyond just doing their business; they involve people both emotionally and intellectually in how they are rewarded, valued and involved. Most of all, the best employers make work a fun place by building community, teamwork and incentive. This dramatically increases the chances of knowledge and innovation being seen as a fun and stimulating experience, while not jeopardising life outside of work.

CHAPTER 10

Protecting intellectual property

'We are moving into an economy where the greatest value is in recipes, rather than the cakes.'
—CHARLES LEADBEATER

Protecting intellectual property requires:

- safeguarding our intellectual rights
- a comprehensive trademark, patent and copyright strategy
- agreements on what can and cannot be shared
- recognising the legal rights of copyright owners
- closely vetting innovation-development firms.

Profiting from your genius

In business there are many people who are ruthlessly searching for a leading edge that will help them profit at your expense. Stealing ideas and diminishing reputations both within and outside the law has now become a fact of life in the knowledge economy.

In this knowledge economy the industries that are creating in-demand assets, such as licensing fees, branding and royalties, have become the movers and shakers. For example, it is estimated that by 2006 half of US workplaces will have a knowledge-generating industry as their primary source of wealth (Stewart, 2001). Here competitive advantage depends on the ability to stimulate and capture knowledge and reduce the risk of losing intellectual assets, talent and know-how. So it is not surprising that intellectual property protection is now a major concern of so many businesses worldwide—particularly given how easy it now is to publish and send vital secrets to a cast of millions via cyberspace or the mass media.

To highlight why the protection of intellectual property is so important let us take the story of retired managing director, Frank Bannigan, who developed the Kambrook electrical powerboard in 1972, which is now common place in most homes. However, as IP Australia says on their website at www.ipaustralia.gov.au, the powerboard was not patented. When it hit the marketplace Kambrook ended up sharing many dollars with a host of other manufacturers. According to Mr Bannigan, 'I've probably lost millions of dollars in royalties alone. When I go into a department store and see the wide range of powerboards on offer, it always comes back to haunt me.'

The lesson of Kambrook is not unique; it is repeated many times a year in most countries throughout the world. Probably the most famous case was the Wright Brothers. Popular history tells the tale of how the Wright Brothers on 17 December 1903 were the first to complete a powered flight. In fact this is not true. It was a little-known New Zealander Richard Pearse who completed the first flight some eighteen months earlier on 31 March 1902 in New Zealand at Waitohi. In fact Pearse completed at least half a dozen recorded flights before the Wright Brothers were ever successful. Sadly for Pearse it was not until 1909 that any newspaper covered the story of his amazing success. By then it was far too late—the Wright Brothers had already gained massive international exposure and recognition. Even now some one hundred years later most people have never heard of Richard Pearse. This story is another example of why it is so important to protect, manage and market your intellectual property and share your success.

So let us begin with some grounding principles of intellectual property management. To win the knowledge game it is imperative that your business takes a series of legal and business steps to protect your genius, whether it is an invention, a trade secret, a brand or a piece of creative work. In saying this, a business should never lose sight of three fundamentals. Firstly, just because you have a registered trademark, patent or copyright it does not guarantee you business success. It needs to be backed up with a comprehensive marketing and business strategy. Secondly, good intellectual property is only a small part of what you need. You must also stimulate and grow a workplace environment that celebrates ingenuity and enterprise as a natural part of the business psyche. Thirdly, be prepared to think well outside your own country to safeguard your interests, and be prepared to register your intellectual property rights in overseas markets.

It is necessary to think deeply about your product, business and market. For example a senior scientist in biotechnology business Gradipore estimates that on average it costs them between US$30 000 and US$50 000 to take a patent application to the right national and international coverage. This cost does not include the cost of redesign and testing of the patent. In one case, where a legal judgment was required, it cost around US$50 000 just for an opinion.

It is clear that the protection of intellectual property needs to be done correctly. It is not something you can normally handle on your own. You will need assistance from a host of people, including government agencies who supervise the registering of trademarks, patents and copyrights, intellectual property attorneys and a host of other professionals who can give advice on funding, marketing, manufacturing and distribution. However, when approaching these people be careful to keep your cards close to your chest and develop relationships based on a need-to-know basis with clearly understood and articulated confidentiality agreements.

When protecting intellectual property you also need to be prepared for some legal ambiguity, particularly when it comes to stopping people from sharing their knowledge. For example, Jac Fitz-enz (2000) in his book *The ROI of Human Capital* says, 'It is relatively easy to slap a brand, trademark, copyright or patent number on a piece of intellectual property. It is a bit more bewildering to find a method for putting one's brand on the human brain.' A judicial battleground has now formed, with lawsuits flying in all directions trying to establish a body of legal precedents for intellectual assets. For example, in the US Apple spent millions of dollars and nearly went insolvent trying to protect its personal computer 'windows' concept against Microsoft, while Sun Microsystems was able to win its case on the proprietary nature of its Java browser software against Microsoft, but it took many years. It is a very tough field but if you get the basics right you will be on much firmer ground.

Consider the common dilemma of a friend—who I will call George. George is a stockbroker in a medium-sized firm in Sydney. At a Christmas cocktail party I raised the idea of sharing knowledge. His response greatly interested me. He said sharing your knowledge may be a very noble idea, but it could mean professional suicide. If you share more than you have to, people will know everything that you know and your security is threatened. Once your knowledge is visible the organisation can protect it and restrict you using it as they see fit. The result is an impasse, where George shares enough to get the job done but probably nothing more. Quite simply, his company is not reaping the full potential of George and his know-how.

If only George could be encouraged to be a little more open, his capability could grow as he begins to review and question his assumptions, relationships and frameworks. No doubt under the current stalemate both parties are losing. Of course this situation will worsen further if George actually does leave and his knowledge has not been captured. This may result in a serious loss of competitive advantage if vital intellectual property and business relationships have not been protected. This is not to say, of course, that George would act unethically or break the law. But it is imperative that every business has counterintelligence measures to ensure that vital knowledge is protected.

One way to protect vital knowledge is with excellent confidentiality agreements for all forms of employment, whether it is contract, full-time or part-time employment. People need to know that they can be employed and leave on good terms, and that the obligations and rights of inventors are safeguarded.

Effective processes must be used to reduce risk. For example, people often have access to important databases, and as a result have the opportunity to download or copy vital knowledge as well as causing possible disruption to services. So you will need to supplement intellectual property strategies with adequate security, such as changing passwords and restricting access. This is particularly important in high staff turnover areas. Obviously at the time of the individual's departure various risk management conversations may need to explore the potential for brain drain or loss of know-how. Examples of questions could include:

- What proprietary knowledge did the employee compile and where is it stored?
- Who are the employee's key customer contacts and business relationships?
- What important knowledge did the person hold and will its loss hurt the business?

You may also take the opportunity to quiz the departing individual about what changes could be made to improve how the business stimulates ideas, shares knowledge and acts on individual know-how. Of course in most situations this is far too late. As was discussed in the last chapter on sustaining and keeping talent, it is much better to explore such topics and the individual's motivations well before the moment of departure actually occurs.

Creating intellectual property does not mean you will automatically own the rights to it. You must take up formal registration if you want the legal rights and benefits of being an owner. You must also apply for each country of interest; you cannot get blanket world coverage. In the case of copyright and circuit layout rights your rights are automatic if you are the author or creator. Be very clear about your intentions and business plan so that you do not fall into the trap of running up a huge bill and an administrative nightmare. In most countries you can now get a provisional patent for twelve months for a nominal fee, which gives you the breathing space to do some homework before the formal patent application process begins. This will allow you to explore the right portfolio of protection. The formal lodgment process usually takes two to three years if everything goes smoothly, but much longer if the application needs clarification or proving.

To sum up, every business needs a combination of approaches to profit and benefit from the genius of its employees. You can start with a stick approach where an employment contract spells out penalties for taking expertise, clients and contacts elsewhere. Alternatively, a business can use a carrot approach where there is a targeted accelerated development program for key people who have vital skills, knowledge and capabilities. This approach builds a business relationship, which recognises talent and encourages people to share more.

The whole field of intellectual property is very complex. To help start you on your intellectual property knowledge journey, try visiting the following websites:

- the Australian Copyright Council at www.copyright.org.au
- the Centre for Law in the Digital Economy (CLIDE) at www.law.monash.edu.au/clide
- copyright and intellectual property rights at www.disastercenter.com/copyrite.htm
- general law resources at www.megalaw.com
- Intellectual Property Australia at www.ipaustralia.gov.au
- the Ministry of Law in Singapore at www.minlaw.gov.sg
- Oz Net Law at www.oznetlaw.net
- the World Intellectual Property Organization (WIPO) at www.wipo.org

The listing of intellectual property definitions in the box below draws on a host of resources from around the world. It is important to double-check the accuracy and context in your region or country. Every country has different common law and statute provisions.

Intellectual property terms

Assignment is when a patent, design, trademark, copyright or trade secret is sold and/or transferred to another party. An assignment must be in writing and be signed by or on behalf of the owner to be legally effective.

Confidentiality agreements are legal documents that aim to protect matters of agreed importance from causing damage and harm, or from becoming public.

Copyright protects the rights of the original creator or innovator of a creative work. It includes tangible mediums of expression, such as a book, screenplay, training module, drawing, recording and broadcast. This is a rapidly changing field and many countries have amended their legislation to have a more realistic coverage within the context of the digital age. As a rule of thumb, copyright does not protect ideas, but rather the way that an idea is expressed. Copyright is designed to protect you both economically (i.e. your economic right) and your reputation (i.e. your moral right). The moral right is much harder to transfer.

Cybersquatting describes the practice of deliberately registering domain names that are the same and/or similar to famous organisations, brands or people.

Design is a feature of shape, configuration, pattern or ornamentation that is applied to a product. The emphasis is typically on the visual appearance like fabric design or the shape of a bar stool, rather than how it works.

E-law is an emerging body of law relating to the Internet and e-commerce. In some cases existing defamation law can be applied to digital communication but there are emerging fields such as domain name protection (i.e. cybersquatting).

Intellectual property, which is sometimes called proprietary knowledge, refers to property of your mind or intellect. In law it gives the right to use and commercialise it, and to prevent others from using and marketing it.

Legal protection applies to a bundle of intellectual property, such as patents, copyright, trademarks, registered designs, confidential information, domain and business names, plant breeds and circuit layouts. It occurs under a range of sources, including common law, infringements of trade secrets, passing off of trademarks and breach of confidentiality agreements. A range of consumer protection and fair-trading legislation usually backs up your legal rights. For a trade secret, the owner must demonstrate that measures were taken to protect it, such as limiting distribution, securing it and appropriately classifying its documentation.

Licence gives to another party the right to use but not own the copyright, patent, trademark or design. The owner normally receives payments or royalties for use based on a commercial agreement. Licences can also be exclusive or non-exclusive in nature.

Passing off is where a person or company is 'passing off' their product or service as those of another person or company, thereby gaining profit from another's good name, and potentially injuring the business or goodwill of the legitimate organisation.

Patents are a monopoly granted to inventors who have created something innovative. In return for the patent, the inventor has to reveal how the invention works. The normal length of a patent is twenty years for a substantial difference in an invention and eight years for a non-obvious innovation of existing technology. The criteria for granting a patent are that it must be able to be manufactured, be new, involve an innovative step and be useful (e.g. protection of new plant varieties). What can be patented varies from country to country—for example, software and algorithms are accepted in Singapore and the USA, but this is not the case in some other countries. In Australia, artistic creations, mathematical models, plans or a purely mental process cannot be patented.

Registered rights are when patents, trademarks, designs or plant breeders' rights (for new plant varieties) are registered with a local country authority.

Trademarks give protection to names, letters, words, symbols, pictures, sounds or smells, or combinations of these. An example is a word like Xenical, which is a distinguishing name invented by F Hoffmann-La Roche AG in Switzerland. Slogans like 'Oh what a feeling', which is used by car manufacturer Toyota, is also a registered trademark.

Unregistered rights are those common law protections such as copyright and circuit layout rights, which cannot be registered.

Getting the basics right

As you would expect, the field of intellectual property and business law is not short on advice. A lot of it is free, while much of it is on a fee-for-service basis. It is essential that you tap into the right resources and get the basics right. Reaping the benefits of your intellectual property protection requires careful thinking, the right level of secrecy and applying many of the skills we have already discussed. So what are the basics you need to consider? The following nine principles will help you protect your intellectual property:

1. *Complete a detailed audit.* Start by doing a detailed audit of the intellectual property you own. You may need external help to do this properly. In some businesses this may be part of the annual planning cycle. Unlike tangible assets such as plant and equipment, intellectual property can increase in value. Look at your financial reporting and list your registered rights, trade secrets and brands; place a dollar value on them. Make sure your staff and business partners understand the reason why the intellectual property strategy is important and why such knowledge is worth protecting. Conversely be prepared to throw out intellectual property that is no longer serving any purpose. Develop an infringement policy if parties break confidentiality or they infringe your legal rights. Seek the advice of an intellectual property expert if you are in any doubt.

2. *Consider the relevance of the know-how to your business.* Any idea for the protection of intellectual property needs to be of business value; otherwise it will not attract the necessary investment and backing. Also, will the intellectual property steer you in the business direction you desire? Does the proprietary knowledge fit the core technology, know-how or capability of the business? What type of professional, logistical and financial support is needed to make it work? Will you be able to support it with the required time and effort?

3. *Think big before you go public.* Where possible avoid talking about your intellectual property until it is registered. Timing is everything. Ensure that your marketing and business dealings do not allow your idea to be stolen and registered in another country before you have had the chance to use it. Careful planning and smart publicity is vitally important. Most of all, think big before you go public. You need to have the right level of security on such services as websites to reduce the likelihood of vital knowledge getting in the wrong hands. If you are not taking protection seriously you may diminish your legal rights at a later time. You will need to be clear about what you can share and what you should own. Remember that being first to the market is only an initial advantage. If you register

the trademark and design in the right way with the right authority, you have the capacity to reap higher rewards. It also helps if you keep a step-by-step, witnessed record from the birth of the idea until the time the idea receives formal registration. A useful tip is when you come up with an idea, mail it to yourself and do not open it when you receive it. This then becomes proof of when you came up with the idea.

4. *Assess whether your idea meets the criteria.* Be clear about whether your idea meets the criteria of being a trademark, patent or design. Make sure you use the on-line search facilities that exist in most intellectual property registration offices. Some skilled inventors prepare their own application, but employing the services of a registered attorney or expert can develop a stronger proposal. Make sure your formal document process ensures that all the correct information is collected and secured. Needless to say shredding or erasing damning and/or vital evidence is a big mistake and could hurt your legal status at a later date.

5. *Ensure you are not infringing the legal rights of others.* Do an advanced and detailed search of existing intellectual property. You have to ensure you are not infringing the legal rights of others. You may need to hire a legal practitioner or search firm to undertake the in-depth analysis. There is now a worldwide database of over 30 million patent documents. This is a powerful source for studying technical trends and competitive intelligence. You can choose to challenge the upcoming granting of rights to another party if you believe it is unlawful. If a patent is challenged, the patent is normally presumed to be valid and the burden of proof is on the challenger. Additionally you may wish to explore a host of private providers that help businesses keep a track of intellectual property approvals and industry-specific research. Two examples of websites that offer services in this area are www.delphion.com and www.nerac.com.

6. *Establish a good fit with your business partners.* Where you need to form business relationships or joint venture partnerships to manage the intellectual property process, it must be based on honesty and transparency. Look beyond just the legality of the arrangement to whether you will be able to work together in business. Be up-front with your joint venture partners, fellow inventors and employees. That way you are better able to determine whether there is a good

fit to the cycle of innovation. Establish clear guidelines on how the relationship will be managed and audited. Secure commitment with non-disclosure agreements.

7. *Market your know-how*. Having done all the hard work and registered your intellectual property, take every chance to market your know-how. The more you promote and market, the more the benefits will blossom, particularly if your customers, suppliers and manufacturers see it as of high value. Even the best ideas can be overtaken if you do not have well-organised marketing and innovation campaigns.

8. *Use your rights smartly*. You can choose to assign or license your intellectual property to another party. This would normally be done if you do not have the time, funding or desire to develop and market the idea. There is a host of providers who could assist you to find a good deal. As in any industry, there are sharks in the marketplace who are very keen to take your money. So be very careful. Make sure you undertake reference checks before you proceed into any formal agreements. This will be discussed further in the last section of this chapter. It is very easy to get paralysed with the excitement of your idea. I know this as an author. We need to keep our feet firmly on the ground, be a little detached and ask who is going to benefit from this idea. Some ideas may sound good in theory but may not work in practice. So be courageous and mature enough to do an independent assessment.

9. *Accept that even the best idea will be superseded*. What was a great idea three months ago may not be so now. Be studious about protecting your intellectual property but do not become subsumed by it. What is more important is that you have a healthy capacity to review your intellectual property. Ensure you are getting the credit you deserve, anticipating and managing risk, and maintaining the right flow of knowledge to grow your competitive advantage.

Confidentiality agreements

A rapidly growing area of practice in intellectual property law is the drafting of confidentiality or non-disclosure agreements. Such agreements can be used in a variety of situations, including arrangements involving employees, contractors, consultants or joint venture partnerships. These agreements are supported by a range of common law rights, including 'breach of confidence', as well as legislation such as trade practices and fair-trading laws.

To draft a workable and enforceable confidentiality agreement, there must be a clear declaration of the specific information that is deemed confidential. This is assisted by a written agreement but it does override the common law doctrine of 'breach of confidence' between the employer and individual. Secondly, in regard to employees there is a strong common law principle of displaying a 'duty of good faith', which restrains an employee from using information that might damage the employer's interests. The 'duty of good faith' is normally covered in the employment contract. Thirdly, the rights of the employer must be balanced against the rights of the employee. An employee must be able to earn a living, using his or her knowledge and skills that they developed during their employment.

Finally a former employee may freely work for a competitor and engage in any activity, which directly competes with a past employer— as long as they do not utilise the former employer's confidential information like a chemical formula or secret manufacturing processes. A well-known case here is that of Jose Lopez De Arriortua and three of his former colleagues who absconded with proprietary documents when they moved from GM to VW in 1993. It was settled out of court at a cost of US$100 million. However, an employee is not prevented from using his or her recollection of commercial information that has not been kept secret, such as names of customers, to compete with his or her original employer.

Specific clauses to include

So what does one include in a confidentiality agreement? To start with, it depends on the context and specifics of the situation, and so it is important to consult a legal professional when considering such an initiative.

It is worth noting that a confidentiality agreement can help to open up conversation rather than close it down. For example, when consulting I often come across team conversations where they are not willing to discuss a business matter in front of me, being an outsider. If, however, it was decided that I needed to be part of a conversation that is commercial in confidence I may need to sign a confidentiality contract.

That way we can continue in a more open and helpful environment. So a good confidentiality agreement may not only safeguard your business, it can open up the arena of discussion.

To assist you draft a confidentiality agreement, listed below are some of the elements you could expect to see.

The elements of a confidentiality agreement

The definition of confidential information outlines the scope, ownership and binding nature of the coverage. It would normally include trade secrets like a manufacturing process, recipes, engineering and technical designs and drawings, product specifications, customer lists, business strategies, and sales and product information.

Understanding the practicalities details in what capacity the information is not to be disclosed and to whom. These obligations may also spell out matters such as setting up a competing business in the marketplace or using confidential information or trade secrets.

Limits on non-disclosure spells out the limits on what is deemed confidential. There must come a point where information is in the public domain or is common knowledge. These boundaries must be detailed.

The length of the term must be long enough to protect the interests of the parties while also not unduly burdening people's rights.

Other possible clauses. There is a host of other considerations that may need inclusion. For example: the rights to amend or even end the contract if both parties agree; the return of confidential material; the options for mediation or arbitration; specific reference to a relevant law or legislation; the rights of injunction, damages or redress if the agreement is breached; and the area of coverage (e.g. a specific market tool or scientific invention).

Copyright in the digital age

One of the most rapidly changing areas of intellectual property is the law of copyright. A major driver is the Internet, which has required most countries to rethink their approach and coverage. For example, copyright legislation in many countries has been recently amended to better reflect trends in on-line transfer of media, entertainment and communication material, providing better coverage on exclusive rights and penalties. This was seen when Napster was forced to restrict access to copyright material via their website. As a guiding principle, once original work is created it is copyrighted and as a result is protected from copying or plagiarism. This typically includes written material, artistic works, musical works, dramatic works, computer programs and compilations.

In recent years there has been significant cooperation and cross-fertilisation between countries to provide greater consistency worldwide. For example, the International Treaty for the Protection of Literacy and Artistic Works (i.e. the Berne Convention) was established to require nations to recognise the moral rights of integrity and attribution in how copyright is protected within their own legal system. The Berne Convention has helped protect economic rights for both local and most foreign owners. The Berne Convention establishes that all things are copyrighted the moment they are written, recorded or produced, and no copyright notice is required. In more recent times a similar agreement called the Madrid Convention, which aims to protect the international coverage of patents and trademarks, has been established.

It is worth noting that there are some subtle variations between the rights of parties such as employees and freelancers/contractors. For employees, if a work is created by them in the course of their employment and as part of the employee's usual duties, the first owner of the copyright will usually be the employer. For the freelancer or contractor, the situation is different. Generally the freelance creator is the first owner of copyright. The person who paid for the work to be made is generally able to use the work for the purposes for which it was created but may not be entitled to use the work for other purposes. For example, a freelancer who created a training manual for a client would be the copyright owner, unless the contractual agreement specified otherwise.

When it comes to the Internet and copyright, there are a number of interesting comments worth making (however, check these observations with a local legal expert in your state or country):

- For work on the Internet, unless a person places words such as 'I grant this to the public domain' you must assume the work is copyrighted.

- US cases are increasingly proclaiming that once information is placed on the public part of the Internet it ceases to be confidential. Of course if it got there by an unlawful disclosure that may be another matter.
- All e-mail you write is copyrighted. However, suing over an ordinary message would unlikely attract any commercial value. Unless the material is secret, or has intellectual property protection, the law normally does little to protect people's rights. When it comes to intellectual property law, computers do not make copies of information, only people do.

Copyright does not stop you from expressing your views on other people's work, only the ability to express the intent or exact wording of the original work and damage the commercial value of it. This helps safeguard the right of the creator to have some control in how their work is used.

Having a comprehensive innovation strategy

In addition to excellent intellectual property protection, the commercial reality of your ideas will come down to the quality of your innovation strategy. Your business may have a brilliant idea but that will not be enough. You will require know-how on how to develop and market it commercially. This could involve a number of disciplines, including research and development, marketing, financial management and manufacturing.

It is of no surprise that developing a new product or service is at the high-risk end of innovation. Very few inventions pay their way. In fact the vast majority of product development in the marketplace occurs when people see an idea and improve on it. Only a small minority could be classed as truly breaking new ground.

When it comes to manufacturing some inventors or creators try to find a manufacturer to do the production under licence, where they pay royalties. But finding such support can be an overwhelming task. To do this you could consider using the services of an invention promotion firm or in the case of being an author a literacy agent. Again one should tread carefully. Some operators who say they are there to help start with a series of glowing remarks about the market potential of an idea and then before you know it their fees get higher and higher. So before getting excited about the hype, do your research on their track record and the legitimacy of their business. One key question you could ask is how many of their clients have made the grade and generated money. Be wary of any unsubstantiated claims; find out what their clients are saying about them. A 'tell tale' indicator of a poor operator is that they make massive claims about your idea without serious technical assessment and want an up-front fee. Avoid paying up-front fees.

Often it is difficult to distinguish between a fraudulent invention promotion firm and a legitimate one. This may be because unscrupulous and honest firms often use many similar advertising and sales techniques, market evaluations and contract strategies. They often use a toll-free number and target mostly independent inventors.

In consumer protection legislation businesses are often required to report on the number and percentage of successful clients—that means the client has made more money than the fees they have paid. Use a reputable attorney or solicitor to safeguard your interests.

To summarise, there are a number of smart things you can do to make the process of innovation a positive and enjoyable one:

- Ask for proof of claims, including special relationships with appropriate manufacturers, before signing any contract.
- Before having a market evaluation report undertaken, ask what specific information will be included.
- Inquire about the total cost of services very early. Avoid paying any up-front fees. The more reputable firms rely more commonly on the royalties that arise from a successful licensing.
- Make sure your patent is watertight by ensuring that no other party has coverage of the idea.
- Check with consumer protection agencies to learn if a business is obligated to disclose success and rejection rates. Rejection rates are a percentage of all ideas or inventions that were found unacceptable. A low rejection rate would indicate that an invention promotion firm is not being tough enough when deciding which cases to support.
- Tune right out of high-pressure sales tactics.
- Contact fair-trading or consumer affairs agencies to learn whether there are any unresolved consumer complaints about the firm.

- Make sure your written contract contains all the agreed terms before you sign. Have the agreement reviewed by an attorney.

Summary

Protecting intellectual property is an essential element of innovation and business development. Whether you are writing a novel, designing a web page or working on the latest advances in biogenetics, take the trouble to understand intellectual property. It is part and parcel of winning the knowledge game. You need to make sure you protect your rights, reap the rewards and minimise risk. You may also need to consider writing confidentiality agreements as well as verifying the claims and reputation of those with whom you are working. Most of all the area can be quite complex—so make sure you are able to obtain the right level and standard of legal advice.

CHAPTER 11

Leveraging digital technology

'I don't understand the technology but you don't have to; you have to understand what it can do for you.'—RUPERT MURDOCH

Leveraging digital technology requires:

- moving past the hype
- shopping around to get the best fit for your business
- creating web gateways of mission-critical knowledge
- tuning into collaborative technology
- careful research and team consultation.

Travelling at the speed of light

As one reads the latest information technology (IT) news or visits a computer store, you cannot help but be impressed by the number of new applications and how fast things are changing. What was state of the art only three months ago has now been superseded. We are living in a digital marketplace that seems to be travelling at the speed of light.

It is natural to feel somewhat intimidated by such huge change, particularly when you feel that you may be falling behind or losing your competitive advantage. This unease is often fed by the unsettling dilemma of whether to invest in new technology or stay with your current platform, infrastructure or system. To use a golfing analogy, digital technology can supply a few additional clubs to your knowledge, learning and business golf bag. However, just because the number of clubs continues to grow does not necessarily mean that your game will improve. We must still perfect the art of using the clubs.

To grow competitive advantage, a business needs to use technology smartly as a way of improving connections and the quality of interactions between the right people at the right time. We need to accept that nothing will ever replace the intimacy and chemistry of face-to-face communication, but what the latest digital technology can provide is the opportunity to connect with new people and thinking twenty-four hours seven days a week. So enjoy technology but realise that we are by our very nature social animals and need stimulation, interaction and teamwork for true learning to occur.

In deciding which technological path is the best, a business needs to go past the hype and pressure of acquiring the latest killer application and learn to ask the right questions. It is very easy to be hooked on the latest features but miss the central point—that is, how can technology help you improve your business performance? Without this focus it is easy to become sidetracked and not reap the benefits you are seeking.

Not surprisingly, when it comes to trying to understand the trends in digital technology many people bury their head in the sand. They prefer to hide rather than have a discussion with a person who may embarrass them with the latest buzzword, brand name or feature. This, of course, is exactly what we should not be doing. We should put any personal insecurity or inferiority aside and go about creating knowledge-friendly systems that really hum. In some cases we may take this challenge on ourselves but most likely it will be with a team of skilled helpers.

A few years ago I attended an American Society for Training and Development conference in Dallas, Texas. A panel discussion on e-learning was held with some of the heavyweights of the field including a key industry researcher. After about twenty minutes of discussion on future trends one of the panellists read the mood of the room and said, 'You may not believe this but we are confused too.' This created tremendous laughter on the panel and a collective sigh of relief from the audience. We all recognised that we were trying to make sense of something that is very difficult to scale, box and package. The fact is that even the experts are confused—so be kind to yourself and explore the business boundaries and trends but do not become paralysed by them. Take a more relaxed approach and open your mind to new avenues and possibilities without the self-imposed pressure of having to find the perfect answer.

To help you begin or continue your own exploration of digital technology, detailed below are five trends that many people and experts believe will have the most impact on knowledge, learning and innovation in the years ahead. The trends are:

1. smarter knowledge platforms
2. digital e-learning blasting off
3. greater personal choice
4. variable bandwidths
5. common standards and protocols.

Smarter knowledge platforms

By 2010 the majority of world businesses with more than five-hundred employees will use IT platforms to collaborate, share and innovate with employees, customers and business partners. These digital platforms will cast their web much further than their existing boundaries of digital support to include people from diverse industries, languages and countries. For example the International Data Corporation predicts that, by 2004, most businesses will include suppliers, customers and business partners in these systems. By 2008 advanced searching capacities and access to remote and wireless devices such as palmtops and cell phones will massively expand the coverage and range of access of people to learning, knowledge and performance systems.

These observations are backed up by the current growth rates of mobile and hand-held devices of 12 per cent per annum. This world growth far exceeds growth in traditional personal or desktop computers and landline devices such as standard telephones. In China alone, there are now more than 150 million mobile telephone users, with a growth rate of 5 million per month. This is amazing given that most of these people do not have access to standard telephones and facsimile machines.

Wireless and mobile access to knowledge via capabilities such as Blue Tooth Technology (www.bluetooth.com) is also having a profound impact on how businesses are behaving, connecting and cooperating. This is now evidenced by a rapid increase in businesses and educational institutions using wireless videoconferencing, e-learning and short message systems in their day-to-day operations. Heineken, Haagan-Dazs, Costa Coffee, McDonald's and Coca-Cola, for example, are now using instant and short messaging systems to support management, customer loyalty and overall productivity initiatives.

This technology means that you no longer need to connect to a telephone line or a personal computer to talk, see and interact with someone. You could be sitting in a park and undertake an e-learning course, be part of a web conference or do a search on the Internet or company database. All you need is the right input device and back-up support, and off you go. Already the total number of wireless devices, such as palm-held devices, wireless connections and mobile telephones, outnumber wired units like personal computers and land-connected telephones—and the trend is set to continue.

During the next few years digital platforms will continue to be more flexible, responsive and intelligent. Internal websites (i.e. intranets) will no longer be an archive of data but will increasingly become a resource full of instant mobile learning, shared productivity tools, performance help and human connection. Digital capabilities such as customer relationship management, intelligence gathering, data mining, web conferencing, sophisticated searching and e-learning will be part of standard web-enhanced packages. For example, call centre staff are now able to action enquiries with the help of instant expert assistance and customer details when they interact with their customer.

Gone will be the days of struggling through countless web pages or files to solve problems. Future knowledge systems will be unified and consolidated to ensure better stand-alone solutions and delivery to all parts of the business. Depending on your business model this will mean improved B2E (business-to-employee), B2C (business-to-customer) and B2B (business-to-business) learning, service delivery and performance.

Digital e-learning blasting off

In the past few years there has been much talk in business about the benefits and growth of e-learning. According to the International Data Corporation the fastest growing e-learning market is Western Europe, with North America still holding market dominance of two-thirds. There are several recent developments that are fuelling these trends. Firstly, the design that is the backbone of much of the e-learning (i.e. learning objects) is now more widely used in a large number of applications, platforms and collaborative technologies. Secondly, advances in authoring languages, natural speech recognition and wireless mobile access has meant many more people are able to participate in this revolution. Finally, the look and feel of e-learning is fast becoming more flexible, engaging and memorable. From a learning perspective there has also been a much higher standard in how the needs of learners are understood, matched and met.

In the years ahead the appeal of e-learning will broaden and expand to many new areas, away from the already popular business and IT skills to new fields such as self-management, financial budgeting, hobbies and career assistance. Again e-learning will not be just a vehicle for delivery of courses; it provides a wonderful opportunity to connect people and foster learning and innovation by a range of services such as web conferencing, discussion groups, chat rooms, courses and telephone link-ups as part of a total business solution.

In the area of customer learning the growth figures are particularly exciting, as the benefits of customer education and assistance are now being realised. Benefits include maintaining customer loyalty with more educative and informative relationships, up-selling to new products and services, and finally being able to reduce the costs in pre- and after-sales support.

As more people become comfortable with the technology, undertaking a two- to five-minute e-learning lesson will be a natural part of daily life, whether you are undertaking home renovations or on the job trying to solve a complex problem. As will be discussed in Chapter 13 on 'Polishing your training performance', modern e-learning is more instant and user friendly.

Greater personal choice

The increased accessibility of the Internet means that knowledge and learning can be twenty-four hours a day, seven days a week—whether you are at home, on the road or in the office. With this comes the increased opportunity to personalise your digital experience. This can be seen already in the world of interactive digital television. Whether ordering groceries, playing games, receiving a music review, sending an email or being part of a chat room, people's choices are highly individualised.

For business, personal choice in the future will mean making sure people are serviced with interesting and useful knowledge. If you fail to do this people will quickly look elsewhere. In most cases they will expect such services for free but will be prepared to pay if the value is there. So whether you are reaching people by a home entertainment system, personal computer or instant message facility, great care must be taken to personalise the information people receive. The more intimate and useful the knowledge, the more likely you will be to grab people's attention. This of course applies to employees as well.

However, in saying this, access does not necessarily mean better learning or greater involvement. The better business solutions will be backed up with professional and personal support from a human being when and if required. This could be answering customer questions, providing e-learning or assisting collaboration on vital areas of mutual interest.

Variable bandwidths

High bandwidth cable access as well as satellite systems are now an essential part of modern business practice. Without such capabilities many businesses are finding it very hard to compete and keep up to date. For example, in South Korea it is estimated that 84 per cent of people will have broadband by 2004. Such growth rates are also being experienced in other developed nations. Of course in developing countries or isolated locations the picture is starkly different, with the vast majority of people still having difficulty accessing a telephone. In the case of South Korea, a major driving force has been active government intervention to subsidise cable in its endeavour to push digital television. Also being a relatively small size geographically has significantly aided the quick uptake, compared with Australia where the growth has been hindered by vast distances.

However, in the short term, business must anticipate that people could be utilising a range of bandwidth frequencies from 28K modems to higher levels. Given this reality we need to position what we package in the right form and in the right media. In the longer term as broadband and satellite access becomes commonplace, the choices and avenues for collaboration, education and connection will expand enormously. I am particularly excited by the potential of using wireless access as a gateway to learning in the next decade—particularly as the cost of remote hand-held devices comes down and access to instant knowledge and information becomes easier and more sophisticated.

As the coverage and uptake of bandwidth increases and the capacity of wireless and wired devices improves, so will the degree and sophistication in multimedia. In the meantime plenty of creativity and imagination is needed to maintain curiosity and interest in the narrow range as well as stimulating the senses at the higher ranges. Closely associated with the emergence of high bandwidth is the ongoing improvement of networks that govern how the Internet works and connects. The current research and development on creating the next generation Internet—the Internet2—suggests that it is expected to operate at least 100–1000 times faster than the current Internet.

Common standards and protocols

One of the most frustrating elements of the digital age has been the diversity of applications, softwares and infrastructures. There has been a saturation of different products, services and labels, which confuses business and inhibits the potential of digital technology. The good news is that in future the choice will be somewhat easier. There has been increased vendor agreement in recent years to develop packages around common industry protocols and standards, thereby improving the capacity for different technology and platforms to work together. Already providers such as Oracle, PeopleSoft, Microsoft and SAP have made moves in this direction. This has meant a greater capacity to improve and expand current systems without throwing out the better features.

An important reference point for protocols for integrating hardware and software is located at the World Wide Web Consortium at www.w3.org. At this site a panel of experts continually reviews and updates accepted industry protocols. One recent tension point in the area of standards and protocols has been the difficulty of cross-platform capability for reading web pages. Microsoft Internet Explorer and Netscape, the two most widely used browsers, have had their own proprietary features and thus there are still differences in the way that each browser behaves for the customer. This is particularly important given that there can be inconsistency in how the web is received depending on the software being used.

Another area of standards is in authoring language. In the future more advanced versions of the authoring language XML will make the role of searching and finding data and knowledge so much easier. Irrespective of the brand of technology that you are using in your business, you will be able to easily link knowledge and combine know-how. In the area of e-learning similar explorations of standards and protocols are also being explored. Again in Chapter 13 on 'Polishing your training performance' the emerging standard for e-learning called SCORM (Shareable Content Object Reference Model) will be discussed.

Finally, a conversation on common standards and protocols would be incomplete without raising the issue of ethics. Given the power and reach of global technology, consumers, lobby groups and governments are now raising enormous concerns about privacy and the rightful use of technology. Expect much tougher and wide-ranging international laws and treaties in the future. Be prepared for a much higher level of business governance in how you link in and use digital technology. This may mean taking a stand on not spamming, or avoiding unsolicited advertising or other unethical practices that may hurt your image, reputation or profitability.

Getting value for money

Having learning and access to knowledge at any time, anywhere and at less cost is a very attractive proposition. The evidence here is compelling. After the initial outlays, digital technology can provide major savings in how you share knowledge and engage learning. You need only consider the savings you could make in travelling costs and reduced downtime on the job to see the potential. There are many successes in the world of business. For example:

- IBM saved $US200 million in one year with five times the training and at one-third of the cost (www.brandon-hall.com).
- Cisco Systems and Dell Computers are close to doing 100 per cent of their training on-line.
- National Australia Bank is expected to save $2 million in the next two years with a blended solution combining face-to-face and digital delivery.
- Procter & Gamble with collaboration technology has been able to secure a 50 per cent reduction in new product concept and development time (www.informationweek.com/758/prga3.htm).
- Sky City, an entertainment and leisure business in Australia and New Zealand, is now able to supply around-the-clock back-up support to resolve equipment failure at a variety of sites using a common knowledge platform.

Steven Melville, the managing director of Ingena, estimates that a large national or multinational organisation can typically deliver anywhere from 50–80 per cent of their learning in a digital manner, generating multimillion-dollar cost savings in the first year alone. Such figures are no doubt impressive and we can expect to see many more businesses lining up to build a faster and more efficient digital system—one that can build talent, and stimulate innovation and stronger partnerships.

However, again a little caution is needed. To grow competitive advantage, digital technology is only one part of the equation. You need to win over people's hearts and minds to digital technology as well. Delivery or accessibility does not necessarily mean that performance improves or better learning is taking place. Just because someone has access to on-line or wireless learning does not mean they will use it. In many ways business must learn the lesson of focusing less on technology and more on human emotion if it wants to succeed.

This observation became clear to me when I helped a close friend do their first on-line e-learning program at home. As a bystander I was curious about the quality of learning and its perceived value. First of all, being new to e-learning my friend found the level of responsibility much greater than what she had previously experienced. She had to take extra time to discover how to use the system, as well as organising her life so that she could fit in her course demands with her other interests. She also had to have the self-discipline to put aside time at home to tap into the service. She claimed that these demands were much greater than she would have encountered in the more traditional face-to-face learning situation. After a while, not surprisingly, she began to lose interest. She also claimed that the material and training on the e-learning package was at times a little silly, cold and impersonal. She began to miss the experience of face-to-face learning and eventually, when it came to the last assignment, she asked me to help her so that the experience could be completed more quickly.

This story of my friend's experience raises a range of issues pertaining to learner initiative, motivation and assessment. In this case my friend did not find it a positive experience and was not keen to re-enrol into anything else even though the service was available for free. If she chooses to do another e-learning course she should probably choose another provider. Of course many of her reactions have a very strong parallel to those experienced in any distance or external education program, such as a traditional correspondence course. However, without doubt, digital technology is placing new pressures on the modern learner, which cannot be ignored. I know there are better examples, but given the growth of e-learning, each business needs to be ready for the real possibility that e-learning may not always help your people or the business. We also need to remind ourselves that we are competing for people's attention. It is not that people are lazy or unmotivated, but they are busy doing other things.

As a postscript to my friend's experience, when the course deadline had passed, we discovered that only 10 per cent of the thirty-five people enrolled completed the scheduled learning on time. This low statistic does again raise issues regarding the perceived worth of the experience and what barriers or obstacles were experienced. In hindsight, there are many things that could have been done to help my friend—for example, starting the course with a face-to-face meeting, praising her more during her progress, coaching her on how to best handle the study and ensuring she had the basic computer literacy skills. As Colin Pitt from St George Bank says, 'some people love it and others don't like it too much, so you will need to have face-to-face learning as well'.

Again remember that the business needs to drive the agenda and not be paralysed by the latest features, tools and content. Your attention needs to be firmly focused on how technology can lead to better knowledge sharing and business performance. As a rule of thumb, at least 50 per cent of the investment of any budget outlay should be spent on research, change management, education and communication. People often make the mistake of concentrating too much on the hardware and software, and not enough on shaping a new attitude.

It is also worth noting that you may not have to spend a fortune to get a suitable system up and running. This is relevant for small- to medium-sized organisations, particularly if the business has low staffing levels or there are already established protocols in how knowledge is shared. In some cases, the platform and infrastructure that drives your service may lie at a remote location and be managed by a third party. In the modern digital era there are increasing choices on how others can help you personalise your approach without you investing in establishing and maintaining the service yourself. Examples could be learning management systems or the hosting of learning portals, automatic administration functions and more sophisticated infrastructure collaboration capabilities such as threaded discussions, chat rooms and file sharing. In this regard a fee will be required and the pricing can vary from a monthly account to an annual fee, but it may well be the most cost-and-resource effective way to proceed. Finally, if you know how the Internet works you will be aware that there is a gold mine of free resources and software available; with a little know-how and help you can make excellent savings.

Building the best system

To leverage the full potential of digital technology it is essential that you hold meaningful conversations with the various parties, interests and customers. It is here where most interventions go wrong. Any change in technology requires an agreement on what needs attention from a wide range of people. This means having a team-based approach to the design, implementation and evaluation. Digital technology should not be an IT project; it must be a business project. As has been discussed, winning the knowledge game is about having a sharp business and customer focus driving the change. You need to bring together people who have a stake in its success, so that vital decisions and system requirements can be discussed. In larger businesses this will often mean setting up a team of managers, customers, and human resources and IT specialists. If you are using external services they must also be part of the conversation. Partnering is the name of the game. You must ensure that the driving issues are shared collectively and key players are actively involved.

These discussions will require skilful facilitation and senior executive backing. Each party will need to understand the specific constraints and opportunities being considered, while current hot issues will need to be clearly understood. You will also need to build flexibility into your plans by ensuring that you have a new digital platform that can be easily updated with changes in software, networks and bandwidth. This means making sure adequate consultation, user support and integration is organised and carried through.

In some cases expertise will need to be hired or recruited to make the process happen. Again the big danger is that the process is highjacked by a single function, person or vendor, and the shared purpose required for committed implementation is lost. Digital technology is too broad and important for that to happen. Business imperative, teamwork and leadership are what matter most.

Here is a list of questions that will help spark your conversations and exchanges:

- What is the business challenge?
- What are the existing technology systems and plans?
- Which capabilities must we develop as a matter of priority?
- What style and type of digital approach do we need?
- What are the learning styles and needs of the people involved?
- What are the benefits to staff, customers and business partners?
- How open are people to new technology?
- What percentage of the budget is spent on new system development?

- What protocols and ground rules are we going to use?
- What are the system requirements?

As you would expect with so much change in digital technology keeping a handle on what constitutes a good knowledge-based digital technology system is not easy. However, pooling together expertise, building shared understanding and testing assumptions is the precursor to developing a better solution.

As standards and protocols improve so will the flexibility to build a better system. Knowledge management digital platforms already include many capabilities, such as:

- access, retrieval and storage of documents
- appropriate security
- communication and collaboration
- competitive intelligence
- content repositories, archives and management
- chat rooms/discussion/file sharing
- course catalogue and on-line registration
- customer relationship management and feedback
- electronic news, content and multimedia feeds
- email and collaborative capabilities
- facilitating and supporting communities of practice
- filtering and upkeep of learning resources
- launching and tracking of learning
- new learning and knowledge creation
- integration of business systems and workflow
- mapping tools that help you find the right person/expert/authority
- performance support
- search and retrieval engines.

As has been discussed, expect major changes in how knowledge is shared. It will be done in a far more entertaining, engaging and immediate way. The whole premise of learning and keeping up to date will have a different look and feel. Watch in the near future how the fields of knowledge management, learning, competitive intelligence, entertainment and customer service will become increasingly merged into one single architecture or platform. For the employee and customer this means immediate access to knowledge that has never been experienced before.

For the record, the current approaches to knowledge management could be broadly summarised as firstly a database approach using providers such as Oracle, Sybase and Siebel, and secondly an archive approach where a business builds an extensive archive of contacts, files and records with a search engine on top of it. As was discussed in Chapter 4 on 'Faster, deeper learning', people can now download vital files and messages from remote locations. In the marketplace there are many commercial and public providers who can help you search and organise your knowledge. If you would like to learn more about this emerging field, visit www.searchtools.com, www.vignette.com and www.broadvision.com.

Of course if a system is full of poor archives and content, wonderful infrastructure will not help you. Remember it is not the glitz that matters but careful planning, consultation and evaluation. As you would expect the criteria for building good digital systems include the common ones of cost and speed but also issues such as the capacity to present knowledge in a variety of short and meaningful ways.

Now more than ever, digital platforms are helping people shape a different approach to their business, fundamentally changing corporate culture and relationships with customers. Pfizer Inc., for example, discovered through searching millions of screened compounds in clinical trials that Viagra had interesting side effects, which generated a new line of investigation. Viagra was originally trialled to fight angina before being used as a sexual stimulant. Similarly, at Accenture preparation for most projects begins by searching relevant information and contacts through their knowledge database called Knowledge Exchange or KX™.

Without doubt, digital technology is having a profound impact on how knowledge is shared, stored and accessed. This new and modern world of cyberspace is one that opens up enormous possibilities for connection, collaboration and teamwork. Gone are the days when a business could rely on its own small network of a trusted few to get things done.

New generation portals

Our discussion on leveraging digital learning would be incomplete without exploring how changes are occurring in the world of learning portals. A learning portal, or what is often called a learning hub or weblog, is a website that customises a one-stop shop of vital contacts, resources, performance tools and e-learning. The term portal reflects a move away from electronic versions of business information to a haven for collaboration and knowledge sharing. Again the facilities can include communication facilities, data stores and software applications. These services could be available by an intranet to people within a business or available to approved external users such as customers, suppliers or business partners. Either these portals are open to anyone who may be interested or you will need permission.

A well-presented and organised portal can provide a gateway to a whole range of people including customers, employees and the community at large. In this context a portal could be defined as any web presence that helps steer people to multiple sources of mission-critical knowledge. The term portal is being used quite liberally and can mean a wide range of things to different audiences, and could be front edge to a system that drives knowledge and innovation. Without getting too caught up on the evolution of language, it is more important to see the underlying trend—that is, the desire to aggregate assistance, learning and knowledge into a central point where important discovery and human connections can be made.

To help you get a sense of what learning portals are about, here are some samples you may wish to visit, which cover a diverse range of topics:

* About—Human Internet at www.about.com
* Education World at www.education-world.com
* IT Skills Hub at www.itskillshub.com.au

Not surprisingly the growth in portal providers has been very high as it helps to simplify and consolidate the best resources and gateways for winning the knowledge game. In many cases businesses have teamed with external third-party portal providers who help to consolidate resources and permit access to vital knowledge and collaboration opportunities. These strategic alliances not only save time, but also help kick-start the creation of a solid framework for learning, discovery and connection. As you would expect, depending on your business needs there is a wide diversity of features and related web-based applications that can form the basis of such a service.

Again it is important to see portals as just another way to win the knowledge game by sharpening your focus and positioning your knowledge. To do this you need a well-hosted solution and the management of it needs to be first class. The advantages of well-designed portals can be numerous, particularly if people are able to get the mission-critical knowledge on learning hot spots. Conversely, portals that lack quality control and fail to adapt to business and learner needs will quickly lose value.

In terms of businesses that use this approach, one notable example is the chemical company Buckman Laboratories. This example was highlighted in Chapter 6 on 'Creating a smarter business'. At Buckman they have built a portal that includes a wide variety of on-line services. These include customer service, technical experts, laboratory analysis, safety and environmental services, product development teams, problem-solving workshops and change management seminars. Further, their Corporate University Bulab Learning Center provides e-learning in a range of different languages, disciplines and technical areas. There is also access to on-line degrees and higher education.

Web-enhanced collaboration

We have entered a new era of cyberspace where collaboration technology will dramatically help us share ideas. With a minimum of a 56K modem you can participate. For example, Procter & Gamble currently use a business system built on Lotus Notes to connect over 93 000 employees. They provide employees with a host of resources from the latest product knowledge, competitor advertising, market news and virtual meetings on the latest hot topic. Tyco Electronics claims specific benefits from their PlaceWare Conference Center have halved the cost per new sales lead, while the preparation and set-up time for long road shows has been reduced by up to 400 per cent.

Like many people my first exposure to web-enhanced collaboration was with Yahoo. There you can join a discussion group, enter chat rooms or create your own discussion space for people to join in, either by open choice or restricted invitation. As I have found out very quickly this service is one of many and there are numerous providers—some with far more advanced features and services. If you are lucky enough to be part of an Internet community you may have access to far more elaborate meetings and collaboration applications, which everyone can use and share at a high level of intimacy and interaction. Some examples include videoconferencing, Internet directories, application and desktop sharing, chat, and visual tools such as mind mapping and whiteboarding. In addition to PlaceWare, other examples of collaborative technology include CUseeMe, WebEx, Telepost, Help Meeting, Evoke, Web-4M and Microsoft NetMeetings. Take a moment to visit netconference. about.com for extensive listings, resources and ideas.

Of course having access to such web technology is no panacea; you will need to learn how to use the innovations smartly. Such services can vary tremendously in price and quality, but without a doubt web conferencing and collaboration can save travel time, help meet deadlines and connect you to a range of people in a variety of locations. In saying this you will need to ensure that people have the right software, platforms and access before proceeding. In the years ahead the uptake will broaden to a wider appeal such as customer service and more general operations when advances in audio and visual functioning become more integrated and seamless.

For me, it is amazing how quickly you learn when you experiment with the new technology. Here are some tips that have come from my involvement in a recent text-based chat session on an e-learning course:

- Set up five minutes beforehand and ensure you have managed your time so that you can concentrate on the proceedings.
- If you have more than three people involved make sure you appoint a moderator. (The moderator is usually the person who calls the meeting.)
- Keep the sessions short (20–30 minutes).
- Set up a formal agenda after consultation prior to the event.
- If you have a question for the whole group or an individual keep it short and sharp. (Again different software has different options and choices.)
- If you have to leave let people know and likewise when you return advise them.
- Keep to strict timeframes with some time upfront to socialise and bond.
- Make sure you follow up the meeting with action plans and outcomes.

Putting your business case together

If you do careful research on your needs and choices you should be well placed to put a proposal together to get the funding and backing you require. If the consultation process has worked well, issues such as system development and managing change will have received a great deal of discussion well before vital decisions are required.

A good proposal not only details the obvious cost–benefit of an initiative but it also helps paint a picture of what might happen to the business if the implementation and roll out is a success. Here I would encourage you to establish a mission statement for your key idea. In fact a mission statement is a great discipline in any project. It should be a short statement that articulates the business, purpose and values for the project. A mission statement helps crystallise your thinking into one distinct statement. A mission statement should answer the following five questions:

1. Why are you here?
2. Who are you serving (i.e. customers, employees, suppliers or business partners)?
3. What do you want people to accomplish?
4. What will keep a person using your service or product?
5. What will encourage them to return?

Here is a mission statement that I recently wrote for my business website at www.alastairrylatt.com:

> The website of Alastair Rylatt Consulting provides world-class assistance to clients and the web community on finding better solutions to the learning challenges facing the modern workplace.

To achieve this mission this website provides a blended e-learning solution to assist ongoing discovery and innovation. Features now include, or will in the future include, a workplace learning Help Desk, Yahoo discussion group, webcam services and e-learning lessons. It supplements my existing services and products.

When it comes to getting backing for your proposal, having sound logic may not be enough. You will need to plead to people's emotions and egos as well. Your business case needs to be tailored to the wishes and personality of your key decision makers. As indicated there is ample evidence that you can sell the advantages of digital technology if you wish to draw people's attention to it. You can supplement this hard data with testimonials, case studies, presentations and demonstrations. Words like return on investment, higher levels of performance, enhancing business capability and throwing out bad systems are likely to get a receptive hearing.

In terms of gaining support, do your decision makers need a short and sweet proposal or do they expect a fuller and more comprehensive report? All this is highly relevant, along with the more emotional reasons for making a decision such as winning, being leading edge or improving one's image and reputation. The fact is that lobbying may be just as important as cold hard statistics. Past experience can be a great help as it can tell you how decisions are made and what the key arguments are that receive high praise. If you get a rejection be prepared to repackage and try again. See negotiation as a process, not as a single event. This may involve better demonstrations and clearer training so people are better able to make a decision.

Most importantly digital systems must be up and running very quickly. Having designers spending two years developing a system is a luxury of the past.

The final format of the proposal will depend on how decision makers want things to be discussed. Listen carefully and package your proposal in such a way that makes the decision makers' job easier. However, do not hide elephants; make sure there is critical understanding on issues such as timetables, resource requirements, downtimes and evaluation. This will help you to save money as well as making a sound investment.

Summary

Digital technology can make a world of difference to the knowledge capability of a business. For your business to reap the rewards you need to go past the hype and explore how business performance can be improved. This can only be obtained by having conversations with the various stakeholders affected by the proposed changes. Particularly important is drawing attention to the social nature of learning and not just the technology. Specific trends that will have a profound impact on winning the knowledge game in the next decade include wireless delivery of learning, smarter and better-integrated digital platforms, learning portals and web-enhanced collaboration. In the next five years there will be profound changes in how people experience and access the digital age in all forms of business, community work and entertainment, whether they are at work, at home or on the road. So be ready and be part of this exciting journey.

CHAPTER 12

Increasing customer loyalty

'Focus on making your customers' lives better. If they can't see that your innovation is going to make their hotel experiences better or their game experiences better or their shoes better, you might as well stop now.'—BETH SAWI

Increasing customer loyalty requires:

- building a positive emotional bond with each customer
- learning how to generate higher customer value
- strengthening cooperation between data mining and marketing campaigns
- mixing digital technology with live customer support
- knowing how you stand on moral and ethical issues.

Improving customer value

Whether it is small business customers at a local pizza shop, the members of a tennis club or users of a large mobile telephone network, customer loyalty is everything. Outstanding customer service requires an attitude that is not aloof, arrogant or out of touch. In essence, a business's success is determined by its ability to nurture intimate, two-way learning relationships with its customers. This is the distinguishing feature in the modern marketplace. We must all be directors of first impressions in every dealing we have each customer. As Esther Orioli from Q-Metrics says, 'customers don't remember logos or catch phrases, the new economy is built on relationships'. To win the knowledge game you must always have the customer clearly in your sights.

If the customer knows about you and you know about them, you are both better placed to share the spoils of exchange. The goal is not about selling for selling's sake or simply giving advice, but it is about improving long-term shared value. This shared benefit far transcends the value of the current transaction. It moves beyond just price to providing strong guarantees, added benefits and back-up support.

In most cases you want people to return as passionate fans who vividly remember their last positive experience. This is vitally important in a twenty-first century e-business model where it is so easy to shop elsewhere or bypass traditional retail and distribution outlets. In most cases people now expect to be involved in a partnership that counts on their input and involvement.

How well a business treats its customers will determine how well the business grows its competitive advantage or advances its reputation. This is increasingly important in a marketplace where people are expecting the very best with no unpleasant surprises. This view is supported by a 2001 Accenture study that found 91 per cent of Fortune 1000 companies said greater focus on the customer service experience and building customer loyalty is most critical (media release, 28 November 2001, at http://accenture.ca).

In modern times business must adapt to a sophisticated and/or fickle consumer who in many cases knows or pretends to know more about your product or service than you do. An example of the power of customer knowledge can be seen in the purchasing of cars. If looking for a car, a consumer can browse the Internet for the exact vehicle they are seeking on the day they are in the market. When it comes to negotiating with a dealer the consumer is then coming to the table from a position of greater knowledge. This shift in consumer power means that often the salesperson or call-centre staff are less informed than the customer. You need only consider how easy it is for a consumer to be in the know very quickly by way of consumer magazines, reference journals, books, networking, web chat rooms, discussion groups and searching the Internet to understand how the power has shifted. Just ask your local doctor about the level of research that some patients do before they walk in the door. They are armed with drug names, side effects and their own medical history. So managers and their staff had better be ready and if nothing else treat customers with respect whether their knowledge is accurate, inaccurate or they are trying to bluff you.

In addition to the shift in consumer power businesses are continually exploring new ways to position their products, services and know-how in the marketplace. The result is a continual battle to influence consumer behaviour and grab new business. This is not surprising, given how society is swamped with so many brands, logos and promotions. Business needs to be far more personal and clever in how it relates to customers. Highlighted below are some of the latest consumer trends. The same message applies to how employees, suppliers and business partners are treated. As Bryan Bergeron (2001) in his book *The Eternal E-customer* says, 'loyal customers are like loyal friends and loyal employees, they can't be bought they can only be developed'.

Some of the latest consumer trends

- Vic Hunter (1997), the author of *Business to Business Marketing,* claims it is 30–40 times more expensive to acquire new customers than it is to manage existing ones.
- On average, satisfied customers tell between one-quarter and one-half the number of people as compared to dissatisfied customers. However, the good news is that if you handle complaints quickly and well, most dissatisfied customers will become loyal again (www.customerservicetraining.net).

- James Rosenfield (2001a) in his article on 'customer focus-pocus' makes the important point that traditionally in industrialised economies, customers tell fifteen people about their experiences. Now with a few keystrokes the customer can tell 150, or 1500 or 15 000 people—not to mention the potential impact a telephone call to a local radio or television station can have on your business.

- People tend to stay with the same brand unless they are dissatisfied. They like brands with a good reputation because it makes them feel safe and helps them manage complexity. This can be seen in the supermarket where the Food Marketing Institute says the amount of time people spend in a supermarket has dropped in the last ten years from an average of 42 to 28 minutes (Stewart, 2001). People are opting to choose a known brand and get out more quickly. This is also the case on the Internet where consumers prefer to use trusted providers such as Yahoo, AOL and Lycos. For example, in Australia in April 2002, 66 per cent of Internet users visited ninemsn.com.au as against 55 per cent one year earlier (article dated 6 December 2002 at www.nua.ie/surveys).

- e-Marketer Inc. indicates that the best click-through rates for e-marketing on websites are now about 0.3 per cent (Rosenfield, 2001b). For example, permission-based email is 3.2 per cent, non-permission-based is around 1.25 per cent and banner ads on web pages are around 0.3 per cent. In more recent times European trials of direct short-message-systems marketing to portable handheld devices is claimed to be over 15 per cent, most likely because it is new and novel.

Six hot tips for better customer relations

We will now explore six tips that can lead to improved customer relations. These tips can not only benefit your relationships with customers, but will also help you in your relationships with employees, suppliers and business partners. For each of these six tips, how well your business learns and leverages its knowledge is central to success.

Encourage joint problem solving

Maintaining high levels of customer value requires ongoing intimacy and joint problem solving. Business needs to move away from a world of just serving customers to one that welcomes feedback and works with others to make lives easier, more enjoyable and more profitable. This requires the utmost integrity, flexibility and empathy. The more you understand the needs and interests of your customers, the harder it will be for other businesses to cash in on your hard work. Learning, education and feedback is the key.

Meet and exceed expectations

Managers need to be skilled in meeting two quite different expectations from customers. The first is the customer's expectation about what will happen next when they acquire your services or products. This is heavily influenced by past experiences and your track record. If you have a good track record you are off to a good start. If you do not have a good track record you will need to address this issue first. Ignoring it will not help. The second expectation is based on how the customer believes your product or service will work in practice. Here you will need to convince them of the benefits, such as ease of use, saving time, money and effort, and the quality of your product or service. Then you will need to back this up with a consistent and high level of delivery. As Dr Ken Blanchard says, 'your job is not only to meet or exceed customer expectations, but it is to create a raving fan'.

Write a customer service objective

Take the time to write a customer service objective, including considerations such as: product or service, the type of relationship you are seeking to deliver, and the qualities of your brand, image or reputation. In shaping your ideas consider:

- What makes your product or service special? What makes it stand out from those of your competitors?
- How could you package your product or service differently?

- What personal qualities will you demonstrate when you relate to your customers?
- What will the service experience be like for your customers?
- What is the biggest challenge facing your customers?
- What is the key message regarding your brand, image and reputation?
- How will you develop your knowledge to meet these aims and goals?

Don't take loyalty for granted

Loyalty comes from long-term collaboration and excellent rapport. This includes viewing people as partners rather than as the opposition. Retention of customers is important; avoiding the loss of customers (i.e. churn) needs to be a primary objective. Avoid spending all your energies on seeking out new contacts and expanding market share. Focus your efforts on improving the relationships with your current customers by better connection, interaction and honesty.

Be thankful for loyalty and do not take it for granted. It is important to understand how your service is perceived and then make it your passion to discover more about your customers. Use a healthy mix of face to face, telephone and digital technology interfaces to keep interest and loyalty. Remember the frequency of meaningful contact with your customers equates to a higher level of loyalty and improved competitive intelligence. In some cases a simple email once a month may be sufficient, while for more valuable customers, sitting down and having a chat might be better. I know of a sandwich shop near my home that organised a Christmas harbour cruise for its customers. No doubt they achieved plenty of return business the following year.

Connect with hearts and minds

Always aim to connect with people's hearts as well as their minds. Personalising your services and brands and making people feel important is vitally important. Using their name, recalling your last conversation or simply smiling can produce wonders. See recovery in service as a wonderful opportunity to improve relationships beyond current levels. All people have legitimate concerns and frustrations; how well we respond to these will determine if we are able to maintain the relationship or lose it. By showing a little more interest and giving personal treatment you will increase the chances of your customer not being swayed to go elsewhere. Ongoing loyalty is based on a strong emotional connection.

Show and feel empathy

Show and feel empathy with the customer by understanding their concerns from all perspectives. See service as an opportunity to build win–win relationships. Seek out those products and services that can dramatically improve customer value. Avoid spending resources on squeaky wheels that customers are not happy about but are willing to accept. The most important goal here is to determine whether you have met the customers' expectations and acted on their feedback. Questions you may need to explore include:

- Does your customer have a voice on how you can improve your product or service?
- Did your business explain all the relevant information?
- Did your business listen to and understand the customer's needs?
- Is there adequate follow up, support and assistance to your customers?
- Does the customer know why you value their patronage?

Strengthening your capability further

Increasing customer loyalty requires excellent planning and a healthy exchange of ideas. The right behaviours and knowledge need to be applied and used. To do this requires building your capabilities to make it easier for people to be your customer. This involves avoiding confusion and frustration, asking probing questions and, finally, establishing a flexible Customer Relationship Management (CRM) system.

Avoid confusion and frustration

Keep your messages crystal clear, simple and user friendly. Build on the strengths of the past as well as making tangible promises for the future. Be ready to provide adequate training, backup technological support and staffing to help the cause. Do not overload your customers with a confusing array of rewards and incentives. Learn why new labels and brands sway your customers away. Position your service narrowly rather than trying to be everything to everybody.

When people ask for help make it easy for them. Give people clear choices. A little common respect can help enormously. If they are kept waiting, let them know how long they can expect to be waiting. Give them the option of speaking to a human being as soon as possible or guide them to a well-maintained and up-to-date Internet site. Consider purchasing telephone technology that enables customer details to pop up when they contact you by telephone.

Deliver the promise on time, on budget and within the specifications outlined, while being open to supplying a few extra positives along the way. Offer creative solutions to help their understanding of products and services. SAP provides opportunities for customers to join a number of business communities at their website. Amazon has a skilful tracking system to continually assist buying decisions, track progress on distribution and repersonalise what the user sees based on past usage. Dell Computers at their website provides customer assistance on how to manage computer configurations.

Ask probing questions

To increase customer loyalty, you need to critically review existing relationships and find better ways of creating value. Here are a number of important questions to explore:

- Who are your top customer groups or clients?
- What is the strength of the existing relationships and what can be done to improve them?
- How can you use existing products and services differently?
- What knowledge about your customers are you 'sitting on' and not using?

By asking these questions you can get a deeper understanding of the idiosyncrasies and needs of your customers. In particular you are able to decipher important issues relating to the quality of sales transactions or after-sales customer service. At the most basic level, each business must scan and know its marketplace. From there you can begin to vary your products and services and build new relationships, ultimately leading to a partnership where both the business and the customer can get help and assistance before it is too late. Consider the following three examples where thinking a little differently helped customer value, service and loyalty:

1. Chase improved the quality of customer service by drawing on the experience of their relationship managers. When the bank launched one of its new services, it increased calls on customers and product sales by more than 25 per cent, leading to an improvement of 15 per cent in the bank's incremental revenues and 40 per cent in its incremental cost reductions (Rollo and Clarke, 2001).
2. Lend Lease Corporation, after better understanding their customer relationships, shifted their core business from building contracting to one involving funds and project management. This led to increased profitability and a different service to the customer.
3. P&O, whose core business was cruise liners, is now a market leader in contract cleaning and catering. In this case a little lateral thinking about their knowledge and capability worked wonders for expanding business potential to a new customer base.

Establish a Customer Relationship Management system

One of the hottest technological growth areas in increasing customer loyalty is the creation of a digital Customer Relationship Management (CRM) system. A CRM system is a knowledge-creation system where you have instant and highly personalised information on key customers, while also having a picture of current business performance.

Historically, CRM systems have typically been for larger businesses, but now they are increasingly being used in smaller operations as costs fall and leasing options improve. In a for-profit business, CRM could be aimed at improving customer yield and customer share, and not the mass cloning of products and services. In a not-for-profit business, the benefits could be about improving the quality of the experience, better hospital care, better advice or better home support for the elderly.

CRM systems can include a range of features including precampaign analysis, marketing to target groups of customers and personalised

campaigns, call-centre management and education, salesforce auto-
mation, product and service configuration, pricing and after-sales
support. Additionally, a CRM system can assist higher standards of
data mining, customer learning and collaboration, as well as on-line
courses and education. These features can also be broadened to assist
suppliers and other people in the web value chain. For example, Cisco
Systems, like many other businesses, gives data on a real-time basis to
its business partners every single day.

As you would expect there are lots of solutions out there. CRM
solutions are provided by a number of vendors including Siebel,
GoldMine, Onyx, Oracle, PeopleSoft, Pivotal, SalesLogix and SAP.

So what does a digital CRM system deliver? In its simplicity a
good CRM system treats all customers with individual care and
attention, recording their likes and dislikes and helping them with better
service including: resolving issues, managing sales and transactions, and
better after-sales support. CRM systems are customer centric. The best
CRM systems are not those with the latest killer application or software,
but those that maintain a positive connection with the customer, while
making employees feel important.

To reap the benefit of a CRM system there are many lessons to be
learnt. A study by the Meta Group found that between 55 and 75 per
cent of CRM systems failed because they were too ambitious and lacked
focus and back-up training (www.metagroup.com). They also found
that CRM systems were often poorly organised and managed, and
unable to provide mission-critical knowledge on trends and behaviours
on a daily basis. As Martyn Riddle from FrontRange Solutions rightly
says, 'if an organisation has bad business practices to start with, the
introduction of CRM technology without reviewing a business plan
can actually speed up the problem'.

As you would expect the best CRM systems have a very close
partnership between all elements of the business. They provide an
excellent linkage and flow of knowledge between goals, operational
constraints, distribution, marketing and performance. The result is
stronger product and service deployment, customer feedback, workflow
and support. For example, in Christmas 2002, the toy department of
the warehouse of one of New Zealand's largest retailers increased its
sales by 20 per cent, while simultaneously reducing its stock levels by
15 per cent.

Some of the common terminology used in CRM systems is described below.

Customer support technology: common terms

Bot is a software robot that creates the impression you are dealing with a human when a customer contacts a business by email or via the Internet.

Cookies technology customises a version of a web page based on a customer's past interfaces with the site—for example, how people navigate, what they buy and what they are asking. This helps customise their interface the next time they visit.

Data mining is a process that examines behaviour, attitudes and transactional data to identify trends, patterns and relationships, which can assist customer service and loyalty. For example, data mining on records of charge cards or smart-card transactions can reveal the relationship between age, sex and the purchase of a product or service.

Data warehouse is a central database that provides authorised users access to all of its customer information. This database consolidates information from a combination of internal and external sources, and acts as a clearinghouse for such capabilities as data mining, forecast marketing and competitive intelligence. This helps to build a more accurate view of customers and their relationship with the business. Current vendors include Oracle and Sybase.

Intelligent agents are programs that perform tasks such as retrieving and delivering information and automating repetitive tasks, such as answering routine customer enquiries.

Web conversion rate is a measure of the number of visitors who initiate a transaction on a website within a particular period of time relative to the total number of visitors who visit the website.

Mining for higher yields

One of the more powerful technological forces in a world of improving customer value is data mining. Data mining explores high volumes of customer information and identifies key insights on customers and markets. The result is improved service delivery and profitability. The need for data mining and understanding your customer base is highlighted by a recent case study by Mitch Rosenbleeth from Booz Allen where one of their clients found 30 per cent of customers created 200 per cent of the client's profits, 50 per cent were not very profitable and 20 per cent actually destroyed profits (www.strategy-business.com). This finding helped raise a whole series of questions on what needed to happen to improve the customer interface.

In saying this, data mining does not guarantee that you will get the right answers. Great care needs to be taken to ensure the right questions are asked and that you are ready to challenge some of the underlying assumptions and theories you may be exploring. Typically data mining provides answers to well-focused questions such as:

- Who are the early adopters of a service or product?
- Which customers are mostly likely to drop their current service or product and shop elsewhere?
- What is the probability that a customer will purchase at least $200 worth of merchandise from a direct mail campaign?
- Which customers are most likely to respond to a particular offer?
- Which demographic is most likely to purchase the latest product or service?

If properly chosen, such questions can have an immediate impact on customer yield, retention and return on investment. It can also directly impact the execution of marketing campaigns and help to influence buying behaviour and maintain customer loyalty, particularly if campaign strategies deliver high value offers and propositions to the right customers.

As one explores case studies of data mining you will soon discover organisations like Scandinavian Airlines, IBM and the Ritz Carlton Hotel, which have carefully managed the interface between data mining and customer relationships over the last decade. The Ritz Carlton Hotel has maintained a database on its high value customers and used it to provide personalised service. For example, let us assume a customer arrives at their Melbourne hotel who likes a fresh fruit bowl in the room on arrival and a glass of Pinot Noir with their room-service evening meal. They also like CNN on cable television. Such precise information is recorded in the database and enables the guest's experience to be met perfectly each time they stay in a Ritz Carlton Hotel anywhere in the world.

Of course such sophistication does not come cheaply. The logic that drives data mining can vary from complex machine learning and fuzzy logic, to the simple matching of patterns and clusters of analysis. It is worth noting that customer data can also be acquired from a variety of other external sources and third parties such as mailing houses, on-line retailers and credit card companies. These can also help provide a host of individual choices, demographics and competitive intelligence data.

Advancing your B2C web presence

Now that we have explored CRM systems and data mining, let us talk briefly about an emerging area in modern business—web-enabled capabilities. Before discussing this latest digital advance, it is useful to step back and explore the strengths of a human being when it comes to increasing customer loyalty. First of all people bring into a customer interface a versatility and the ability to interact. This is very difficult to mirror or better using technology. However, in saying this, having a person answering every enquiry can be quite expensive per contact, particularly if you want to save time and money in handling routine enquiries on a twenty-four-hour seven-day cycle. Continual person-to-person contact can also lead to staff burnout as well as an increased likelihood of inconsistency. Keeping people up to date and informed is also a huge challenge, particularly in a high growth or rapidly changing consumer market.

As a result deploying B2C (business-to-customer) web technology is seen as a way of reaping the benefits of a human touch by supplementing people contact with very interactive, fast and less error-prone digital support. As can be seen in Internet banking, the transaction price for the customer is cheaper and they can do transactions in their own time. It is expected that as connectivity and bandwidth improve we will begin to see more 3D, e-learning and virtual shopping as a regular feature on the Internet.

Bryan Bergeron (2001) in his book *The Eternal E-customer* discusses the emergence of what he calls Emotional Intelligent Interfaces (EIIs).

Here customer email and web-based enquiries are answered by a software robot with empathy and emotional connection. The result is that the customer is under the impression that they have been dealing with a human when in fact it is a computer surrogate. In the past this capability has largely been unsuccessful. For example, in 1995 Microsoft launched an emotional interface called BOB. The BOB system was used to respond to customer enquiries by email and chat in a somewhat emotional and empathetic way. However, most people found the persona of BOB somewhat condescending, patronising and insulting. Since then there have been many advances, particularly in the more routine conversations using natural voice recognition. In more recent times the Australian Racing Authority (TAB in Queensland) has been using Natural Language Speech Recognition Technology for placing bets on races. It is claimed that about 95 per cent fewer calls need to be passed on to human operators (*Marketing and ebusiness,* 2001a).

It will be interesting indeed to see how this field develops. No doubt it is both exciting and somewhat controversial. I know that when I recently called for a taxi I was dismayed to have to talk to a computer, but the system worked perfectly.

Taking an enlightened stand

There is a huge flipside to the whole debate on technology and the drive towards customer loyalty. The fact is that many customers lose out where a business is only interested in the crème de la crème of the marketplace, or are not interested in investigating how existing customer relationships can be improved. Often commercial realities dictate that only a select few customers are given preferential treatment. In many cases businesses are happy to have unsatisfied customers and still make huge profits from a few. Make no mistake though—current advances can discriminate against the least valuable customers unless a stand is taken on the grounds of moral responsibility or social compassion. Efforts must be taken to truly understand how each customer is benefiting or alternatively how they are aiding or inhibiting your business performance.

James Rosenfield (2001a), in an article on 'customer focus-pocus', says that in many cases customers are being plundered, manipulated and encouraged to move on. He also says that there is no evidence that good customer service and customer satisfaction leads to profitability. The fact is there is a lot of evidence to show that the opposite is true. This conclusion is supported by a Baum et al. (2000) study, which found high performance in technology and customer satisfaction does not necessarily translate into higher profitability.

Given this evidence it is not surprising that there is a groundswell of public opinion screaming for a much better deal for customers. International groups such as J18 and movements against corporate greed and fair trade are a few examples of such lobby groups. It is early days but there are some examples of businesses taking a more responsible stand. For example, banks are now offering more choices to low-income earners.

In the next decade moral, ethical and social issues will become vitally important in growing customer loyalty and succeeding in all forms of business. If the purpose of your business is solely profits, you will need to take a radically different approach and incorporate a more compassionate and caring community-focused perspective if you are going to grow competitive advantage in the long term. It is not for me to say how to live your life or run your business—that choice is yours. However, I do think that the tension between improving customer loyalty and business success cannot be ignored. Customer loyalty can go hand in hand with a more enlightened stand where excellence also means good ethical conduct and social responsibility.

What is making the transition difficult, particularly in the corporate world, is that senior executives are continually being rewarded for cutting costs and increasing shareholder value at the expense of customer service, employee well-being and better learning. As Dr David Morgan, the CEO of Westpac, said in the *Sydney Morning Herald* in October 2002 after his company outperformed the Top 100 companies in Australia in the area of Good Reputation, 'in 1999, when Westpac had to announce a record profit level, we never had the community more dissatisfied with us, we never had our customers more dissatisfied and staff morale was never where it should have been'. Other companies to perform well in the Good Reputation index in 2002—incorporating criteria in employee management, social impact, environmental performance, ethics and corporate governance, financial performance and management, and market focus—were Australia Post, Energex, Queensland Rail, Holden, IBM Australia, Toyota, Ford, Shell Australia and the ANZ Banking Group.

Summary

One of the biggest drivers for improved performance and innovation is increasing customer loyalty. This is based on the value proposition that it is far more expensive to attract new customers than it is to keep your existing ones. The higher the 'personalisation' and 'customerisation', the more likely it is that your business will improve customer retention in the modern e-business era. Businesses are increasingly using Customer Relationship Management (CRM) systems, data mining and B2C web technologies to streamline and improve exchanges with the customer. Again knowledge and the use of it is a major lever in how well a business grows and sustains competitive advantage. However there are no short-term easy gains; it takes a commitment to service, ethical practice and discovery.

CHAPTER 13

Polishing your training performance

'Don't surprise people with content; surprise them with process.'—ERIC JENSEN

Polishing your training performance requires:

- designing training based on the needs of the learner and the business
- creating e-learning know-how
- sampling and exploring new forms of digital learning
- stockpiling small chunks of reusable business knowledge
- combining traditional training with new digital delivery.

Breathing life into business learning

Business success requires a training effort and learning process that inspires imagination, discovery and performance. Successful training programs address business needs as well as the aspirations and dreams of people.

At the business level, training often starts by addressing gaps in knowledge that need immediate or urgent business attention—for example, lack of expertise in technology, managerial systems, skills or attitudes. Training can also seek to improve the quality of succession planning, career development and lifestyle by helping to address burnout, morale issues, and relationship and/or teamwork skills.

At the personal level, learners need to be convinced that there are tangible benefits in doing the training. For example, will the training build self-worth and inner confidence? Will the training be worth the investment of time and effort? Will the learning be useful? If these needs are neglected, your training effort could well be wasted.

Without doubt in the modern knowledge era there are many pressures that can assist or frustrate any training effort whether it is on-the-job, classroom or e-learning. If our goal is to breathe life into training we need to help people understand the promises, doubts and vulnerabilities that come with learning. We see this most when people are stretched outside their zones of familiarity or comfort. It is in this domain where the leaps in our capabilities can be highest, but also where the greatest emotional and practical support is required. At these times we need to draw on our personal reserves and the support of others to succeed. Whether it is rethinking our strategy or just being a little kinder to ourselves, we need to take positive action to overcome the struggles we face in the learning zone. In practical terms this means providing emotional and intellectual support at every opportunity.

There is often talk in training circles that learning must be fun; in reality it can often be the exact opposite. We all have to be ready and willing to help each other make the transitions and learning we desire. Instead of viewing training as a purely logical process, we must encourage people to notice and respond to the moods and emotions they will face. For example, what tactics can learners use to motivate themselves when they need to learn more? Such inspiration and self-management is priceless when it comes to the development of skills and know-how. Additionally, make sure there is excellent practical and emotional support to help people and teams learn smarter. For example, with digital learning, clear guidance on computer awareness, tutor availability and the right software and operating systems is essential. More traditional training can be backed up with tools, learning books and management support.

Helping a learner learn and building training performance has been a theme of many of my past books and articles, most notably *Learning Unlimited* and *Creating Training Miracles,* which I wrote with my colleague Kevin Lohan. These books highlighted the key design elements of a successful training program:

- Give your training or learning an exciting name that grabs attention.
- Start your training by:
  — explaining why the learning is important to the learner and to the business
  — sharing a real-life story that demonstrates the reality of the benefit
  — painting a BIG picture to show how the training fits with other responsibilities.
- Stimulate curiosity and thirst for learning by creating plenty of opportunities to apply and practise what is being discovered.
- Highlight relevant stories, examples and simple frameworks to aid recall and application. Review and celebrate to the maximum.
- When the training is completed do not leave things to chance; make sure there is adequate coaching and tools to assist and reinforce new skills.
- Evaluate and improve the process for next time.

Apply these principles in all your training efforts and you will have more success in face-to-face training, on-the-job coaching and/or e-learning.

Surrounding the whole conversation of breathing life into the learning process is the assumption that for training to work it must consider and adapt to the unique learning styles of the people involved. Again the topic of learning style has been a major theme of my previous books and I do not intend to revisit those ideas now. To help you explore learning theories you may wish to visit http://tip.psychology.org/ or www.patsula.com/usefo/webbasedlearning/.

When it comes to discovering about learning theory and styles I have found the work of David Kolb, Peter Honey, Alan Mumford and

Ned Herrmann most relevant and useful. Other related fields that you may wish to explore include: instructional design, neurolinguistic programming, competency-based training and of course web design.

Helping the e-learner

As has been highlighted, learning by the web and other digital means has given people more ways to acquire knowledge and capability around the clock. Whether it is doing an on-line course, participating in a web broadcast, on-line chat, linking into a company e-library or viewing a CD-ROM, the choices and avenues are continually expanding. The result is good news for learners and business because employees, customers, partners and suppliers have a much greater chance of keeping up to date and trained.

The reality is digital learning or e-learning is no different from any other form of learning; it needs to be well organised and structured to succeed. It requires careful thought and planning about the business needs, audience, the delivery, the content and evaluation. As has been previously noted though, the delivery of information to a person's computer or palmtop should not be confused with learning. Just because someone has access to the latest e-learning package does not necessarily mean they will find the time or be motivated enough to check in and do what is required. Within these broad headings you will also need to consider issues such as the choice of technology and navigational strategies.

Additionally, you need to assess whether the knowledge is relevant or useful. In many ways digital learning comes with a much higher level of self-management and responsibility than has existed in the past. So before becoming too carried away with advances in training using digital technology, make sure that the needs of people have been addressed and that digital learning is the best method for your business. Only then will we begin to see a large-scale revolution in training performance.

A well-designed e-learning lesson can stimulate the senses by making the training experience interactive, relevant, engaging and entertaining. Done properly the benefits can be astounding. KPMG calculated that to train 22 000 employees on e-business fundamentals by traditional face-to-face methods would take three years. However, by investing

$US3 million in e-learning, they could train 8000 employees in eight weeks (www.internetweek.com/indepth/indepth110600.htm). Counterbalancing this outstanding result is a clear industry observation that many e-learning initiatives fail to meet business expectations. Common reasons include being too preoccupied with rolling out content and being fooled by outrageous expectations of cost savings and return on investment. In fact a 2002 UK study by THINQ indicated that 65 per cent of companies are not making use of e-learning to fulfil internal training requirements. In smaller companies the figure of non-involvement was much larger at 78 per cent (www.thinq.com/pages/presse_2002_0729.htm). This study summarised a common perception that people felt that on-line learning is a stand-alone addition to traditional training, when in reality, it needed to be integrated into an overall learning approach.

As you would expect, changing from a more traditional form of learning to e-learning will generate resistance from some people. Many still prefer the old model of on-the-job learning and attending live classes. Alternatively, there will be people who wonder what all the fuss is about and will jump straight in. Also you may well find that the resistance does not come from the learners alone but from the trainers or designers as well. A trainer who loves to present face-to-face may loathe getting involved in web-design technology. If your business wants to move along the road to more e-learning it is quite likely that you will need to bring together an array of new talent to steer training in a new direction with web designers and qualified e-learning professionals being part of the team effort.

Additionally in larger and medium-sized businesses, functions such as human resources, training and IT may need to reinvent themselves and let go of outdated thinking before the benefits of digital learning can be gained. So be wary of classic delaying and avoidance tactics like stalling, not taking it seriously and/or putting in a token effort. Encourage people to do a demonstration as soon as possible. You should not be seeking perfection—just a solid start. Aim to build confidence, expertise and early success.

Like traditional training, digital learning is only limited by your creativity. Whether creating checklists, writing stories or holding one-on-one coaching sessions, there is a wonderful opportunity to thread higher levels of competency and thinking into what a person may experience through digital technology. In many cases a bells and whistles approach may be too much and simple graphics and text would be sufficient.

To help you build the case for digital learning, listed below is a series of questions to consider. There is also a glossary of some of the current digital learning terms. It is worth noting that the terms on-line learning, e-learning and digital learning are often used interchangeably in the literature and industry commentary. Always check the context and nature of technology when you hear or read these terms. Current software products that can aid e-learning and web page design include: Dreamweaver, Microsoft FrontPage, Fireworks, Flash and Microsoft PowerPoint.

Building a business case for digital learning

Kick starting your case

- Which hot business issues could be used to showcase digital learning?
- Which learners are technologically prepared?
- Do you have senior and line management backing?
- Which pressures exist that are making the commitment difficult?
- Do you have a champion of the cause?
- Is the message of 'Why digital learning' getting out there?
- Do people have the knowledge, funding and equipment to undertake such a commitment?
- Have the costs, benefits and risks been clearly explored?

Building momentum for your case

- Are you supplementing the digital push with other sources of inspiration, such as newsletters, email reminders, demonstrations and fliers?
- Do managers, mentors, coaches and trainers encourage change on the job?
- Can you produce evidence that indicates which parts of the business are exploring and/or using the new technology?
- Are people getting an opportunity to put into practice what they are learning?

Generating value

- Is the usage and application of new technologies noted, rewarded and acknowledged?
- Is the digital learning seen as meaningful for both the individual and the business?
- Is there a clear linkage between what is being learnt and the needs of the individual and business?
- Are you capturing stories of how the new approach is helping new connections, improving know-how and helping the business?
- How do you propose to track future activity, contribution and usage?
- Are people giving and getting feedback on how the process could be improved?

Digital learning glossary of terms

General terms

Asynchronous learning is an e-learning event that does not require participation of people at the same moment in time—for example, voice mail, email, file sharing, threaded discussions and interactive voting.

Blended learning is a training program that combines technology-delivered learning with traditional methods, such as face-to-face instructor-led classes. It could also include combining e-learning with other approaches, such as Knowledge Fairs, Open Space, mentoring and reading books.

Blog (weblog) consists of regular journal-like entries posted on a web page for public viewing. Blogs usually contain links to other websites along with the thoughts and comments of the host.

CMS (content management system) is a software application that streamlines the process of designing, testing, approving and posting content on web pages.

HTML provides the code to enable browsers across platforms to display text and graphics, and to create links between web pages and links within pages. It provides the instructions for browsers such as Internet Explorer and Navigator.

JavaScript is a programming language that allows authors to create more stimulating, effective and interactive web pages. Examples include roll-overs and pop-up menus.

Learning object forms the basis of e-curriculum design. It is the smallest chunk of information that can stand alone with meaning. Think of a web page as a learning object. Other terms used here include educational objects, content objects and nuggets.

LCMS (learning content management system) is software that allows trainers and training directors to manage both the administrative and content-related functions of training. An LCMS combines the course management capabilities of an LMS (learning management system) with the content creation and storage capabilities of a CMS (content management system).

LMS (learning management system) is software that automates the administration of training events. The LMS registers users, tracks courses in a catalogue and records data from learners. It also provides reports to management. An LMS is typically designed to handle courses by multiple publishers and providers. It usually does not include its own authoring capabilities; instead it focuses on managing courses created by a variety of other sources.

Synchronous learning needs to be undertaken in real time with others to ensure immediate two-way communication. It includes holding meetings by videoconferencing or audioconferencing, using webcam or conducting live chats on a website. (It is the opposite of asynchronous learning.)

Threaded discussion is a series of related e-messages on a given subject, including the original message and subsequent replies. It enables a focused discussion on an issue or topic. It is often used in e-learning and virtual teams in the form of discussion groups.

Virtual classroom is a delivery of scheduled learning at multiple classrooms via a networked solution at the same time.

XML allows you to describe data and its structure. It works with HTML to assist tagging and linking of information and data. XML is now firmly established as the preferred option for digital learning because it aids advanced search and find capabilities.

Building websites

Active server pages (ASPs) are one of the most popular Microsoft applications for creating a dynamic website and enhancing interactivity. Typically you will need some knowledge of HTML and SQL to benefit, as well as a Microsoft operating system.

Common gateway interface (CGI) sets the rules on how a web server talks to a program. It is used for guest books, hit counters, shopping carts, filling out forms and message boards.

Cold fusion creates a data-driven website. Cold fusion could be used to drive an e-zine (i.e. an electronic newsletter) service. Again you will need some knowledge of programming languages to benefit. Another product that performs this service is Dreamweaver Ultra Dev.

Java server pages (JSPs) are another avenue to create dynamic websites. JSP uses Java (one of the most popular web programming languages). Java and JSP will run on almost all major operating systems.

Exploring e-learning courses on the Internet

Exploring e-learning courses on the Internet can be both exciting and daunting. Here are a few tips to help you get started in this emerging area. The focus here is on getting the most value out of courses that are available on the Internet. Collaborative and other forms of technology have already been discussed in Chapters 11 and 12.

To get a quick feel for what is available on the Internet, look at the following sites. These were recommended by Tony Whittingham, lecturer in an e-learning class at the University of Technology in Sydney. The sites include:

- www.aquinas.edu/homepages/millemar/AT161
- iris.nyit.edu/~tdiener/index.html
- home.sprintmail.com/~debflanagan/main.html
- www.actden.com/pp
- cbae.nmsu.edu/~dboje/sbc/pages/page3.html
- www.openday.uts.edu.au/tour.html

If you have a topic of interest start with an Internet search to see what is currently listed. It is a good idea to always view some free samples or live demonstrations before you make the decision to proceed. This will give you a look and feel for the quality, and any software or hardware you will need. You can also evaluate the product and service before you start. Here are some samples of on-line e-learning course providers:

- American Media Inc.: www.amitraining.com/demos/channel
- Barnes & Noble University: www.barnesandnobleuniversity.com
- Click2learn: www.click2learn.com
- Digital Think: www.digitalthink.com/catalog/
- TAFE New South Wales On-line: www.tafeplus.com/
- the University of Southern Queensland: www.usqonline.com.au

When choosing a course, consider a list of criteria including cost, length of training, structure, interactivity and flexibility. You will also need to check the software and hardware requirements, backup support, instructor expertise, trainer availability, feedback on learning undertaken and guarantee.

If you decide to undertake e-learning discuss your schedule with your manager, co-workers, partner or family at home. Discuss your commitment and what support you may require. For example, if you are using work facilities, having some quiet time on the job will help. You will also need to be considerate of your colleagues if there is a video or audio component. It is helpful to commit to a routine to do your e-learning, whether it is first thing in the morning or late in the day. Choose whatever works for you and your schedule. If your e-learning is in the form of direct performance support like an on-line Help Desk, explore a little about the background and intention of the system before you start. This will help you gain the most value from the support you are receiving.

If you are a novice, find a buddy who can help you with some of the technical aspects of e-learning. Whether it is a course provider, your IT contact or web designer, they should be able to help you navigate the system and support you with any extra software or plug-ins you may need.

See this new form of learning as an exciting way to make connections and friends. Take the opportunity to chat with other learners, either face to face, at peer learning sessions or as part of a discussion group on the Internet. Be the initiator—passively waiting for the answer will not help you. Be assertive and explore the unknown, while being respectful of the time and energy of others. The eventual success you have will be based on the quality of the interaction, debate and sharing, not the technology.

Set realistic goals and do not overburden yourself. Find a healthy balance between work, leisure and learning. Do your e-learning in manageable chunks—20 minute pieces is a good start. If you find the leap to web-based learning too much consider doing a course at an evening college on surfing the Internet before getting into e-learning. You will find better e-learning providers, and hosts will give you an introduction into the functions and applications of e-learning before you start your course. Take advantage of these resources.

Finally, make sure you review what you are learning. Keep a Learning Journal and build on your own personal archive as you proceed. And, do not forget to celebrate along the way, whether it is buying yourself a cappuccino or sharing what you have learnt with others. If you find the course lacks entertainment and quality let the course provider know. Feedback is essential if the world of e-learning is to improve. A good design should be much more than e-reading; it should be interactive, enjoyable and relevant.

Fundamentals of modern curriculum design

Good e-curriculum is much more than just dumping people with text and nice pictures. It provides highly efficient and customised grabs of instruction. Excellent e-curriculum is rich in learner-focused material. Irrespective of whether the instruction is delivered by high bandwidth or a telephone line, the learner should receive relevant and attention-grabbing content, which helps take them on a knowledge-enhancing journey.

To understand how this is done it is important to grasp how digital training design has fundamentally changed into a learning–object approach. Using advances in XML authoring language and agreed industry standards, modern digital training is designed around small pieces of 2–15 minute instruction. Each piece of instruction is independent, reusable and linked to carefully designed search and find capacities. This learning-object strategy helps move the e-design from large inflexible masses of information and instruction to one that is easily revised, searched for and modified. Additionally, the learning objects will easily integrate into most forms of digital technology delivery whether it is a web page, instant message on a mobile telephone or a CD-ROM.

Training is no longer created just as courses. As Elliott Massie, a leading authority in e-learning says, 'technology-delivered training is now assembled, not authored, from large reservoirs of content presented to the learner. More emphasis will be placed on building knowledge bases that can be published on the fly.'

The consequences of this learning-object approach to winning the knowledge game are profound. For the learner this approach helps with consistency and personalisation, while for the business it means developing a structured approach that can easily be adapted to different needs, media and learners. Smartforce, a leading worldwide training provider, claims to have over 20 000 learning objects on a cavalcade of topics for business.

Driving much of the industry reform in learning objects is SCORM. SCORM is an initiative of the Advanced Distributed Learning Network, and stands for Shareable Content Object Reference Model. SCORM is a collection of standards and specifications that sets the foundation for better unity in design, assessment and profiling of digital learning. For more information about SCORM visit www.scorm.tamucc.edu and www.adlnet.org.

When you think of digital learning, think of small chunks of information or instruction. The emergence of learning objects not only impacts digital learning, it will also in the future shape how face-to-face training or on-the-job coaching occurs as managers search out and include learning objects in their lesson plans. Look at your current archives of resources and learning to see how you can stockpile a collection of your knowledge for future use. In this regard one of my clients in local government is currently creating an archive of over 1200 learning objects to assist a service initiative. Their goal is to create a web presence that will provide around-the-clock service, help and training.

The design of learning objects would usually include various elements, such as a short overview, a series of instructional pieces, assessment and summary. The design should encompass a series of interconnected training and assessment processes. The type of learner assessment will depend on how the learner is progressing and what material is included. For example, dealing with concrete facts and procedures or developing capabilities in concepts and processes will require different design elements.

One field of knowledge that is helping the growth of learning objects is competency-based training. During the past two decades many industry and government bodies have established thousands of skills standards, ranging from pastry cooking for chefs to risk management for managers. So do not reinvent the wheel; see what public information you can acquire or purchase. However, e-learning is not just about buying content; you need to back it up with the right business case, design and system.

In regard to authoring or designing it is also important to recognise that not everyone will have the skills and motivation needed. For example, a content expert may be well versed on what needs to be taught, but may have neither the time nor the motivation to do the design. Normally an experienced e-learning designer best performs e-curriculum. This will release the subject matter expert to be more directly involved in other roles such as sponsorship, mentoring and collaboration.

Here again you will need a team effort to succeed. The final design can only be decided upon after holding conversations with business managers, customers, decision makers and vendors. Only then will you have a clearer picture of the content and system design you require. Such conversations do not end at the design phase but continue well into the implementation and beyond. Who does all this work will depend on your capability, time and desire—meaning it could be a combination of an external vendor, responsible course provider and your business web designer.

Having some grasp of modern curriculum design, your attention needs to shift to how a digital training system is coordinated. Normally all of the learning objects you have created are placed in a manifest computer file, which is then managed by a learning management system (LMS). Depending on your budget your business could build your own LMS or have it provided by a third party. For most small- to medium-sized businesses, the third party option is the only realistic one. Before jumping in and acquiring or building a LMS, be careful to ensure common mistakes are not made. Firstly, the LMS must fit your business culture, IT set-up and technology. Make sure you clarify your intentions and expectations. Ensure there is a plan including clear links to your business plan. Secondly, do not go for the cheapest; go for the most value, as there is often a huge difference. Make sure that the LMS is SCORM compliant and scalable. Ask for demonstrations on how vendors and providers are meeting this standard. Finally, do some reference checks with past clients to ensure your vendor is a proven performer. The best way to do this is to find a similar style or sized business to benchmark potential suitability with your operation.

In terms of how long it takes to develop digital instruction, the estimates vary tremendously. If we take one hour of instruction in a classroom, it typically takes around 20–30 hours to do your preparation from scratch. When it comes to digital learning the American Society for Training and Development suggests the ratio can soar to 300 hours depending upon complexity of graphics and simulation, the level of interactivity and the testing required, and of course the level of expertise of the designers and developers. Additionally if you have to start from scratch on the content your time investment will be higher. Meeting industry standards such as SCORM also takes time. For a seasoned professional with the right training, content and software, still expect an investment of between 50 and 100 hours per finished hour.

Blending your overall approach

In exploring the field of training, one guiding principle seems to shine out. No single solution is perfect. You will need a combination of different traditional and digital strategies if you want to improve your levels of performance and knowledge.

In the modern knowledge era, digital learning is providing more sophisticated ways for people to share and learn together. However, digital technology only works when supported by outstanding design, technical back up and human support. As highlighted in several industry studies the digital learning revolution has hardly begun. Statistics on people who are currently undertaking e-learning show that the figure is still well under 10 per cent. The vast majority of those connected to the Internet are opting for email, chat lines and information retrieval rather than choosing web courses and collaboration capabilities. It is still early days.

Conversely, if a business feels they can survive purely on the merits of technology they will struggle to gain competitive advantage. The Masie Center in the US conducted a worldwide survey of 2119 people (www.masie.com). It found 88 per cent of learners and 91 per cent of managers wanted a trainer assigned to their e-learning experience. Further, 62 per cent of learners and 63 per cent of managers would be more likely to select an e-learning class if a trainer were part of the package, either via email or threaded discussion. So, put simply, people want skilled humans to answer questions and provide emotional support and not just the technology.

In saying this, accept that a blended approach is most likely more expensive and you may well lose some of your cost savings from rolling out digital technology. However, a well-coordinated and blended approach will pay off with greater learning and business improvement in the long run. As the director of TPI, Ronnie Stronge says, 'our challenge is how to bring all the elements together in the best combination'.

Finally, look for short bursts of stimulating and relevant training. Shorter duration face-to-face classes and interesting discussions combined with pre-class and post-class learning guides is a more common model now being deployed in best practice cases. Most of all seek to create a spirit of buzz in the learning with a host of different ways to stimulate interest and collaboration. Here again the sky is the limit, whether it is creating a competition, working on a joint puzzle on the Internet, or designing a knowledge-sharing experience.

Summary

In modern business, training must be increasingly clever in stimulating curiosity, buy-in and application. You need to surprise and excite people with a healthy mix of digital delivery and traditional face-to-face. We must not confuse access with learning. Polished training combines delivery with outstanding support and assessment. For some the transition to e-learning is easy, while for others it could be highly stressful and unsettling. As a result e-curriculum needs a design that is based on excellent consultation with business managers, customers and subject matter experts, while also understanding human emotion, desire and willpower. One major influence on modern training is learning objects. Learning objects are small chunks of reusable and replaceable pieces of know-how that form the basis of most modern digital learning. Here again the best results only come with an integrated approach, combining clear business needs with well-chosen training and support. It is only then that the benefits of growing competitive advantage will be realised.

PART 3

Ensuring lasting success

Having invested so much time, effort and resources in opening hearts and minds and to growing your competitive advantage, it is imperative that you back it up with the right formula of evaluation, measurement and review. To do this each business and its people must examine the quality and performance of its knowledge. This ongoing inquiry will include a number of important reviews: firstly, are your existing approaches having the desired impact for your business, customers and society? Secondly, is your capability and know-how adapting to the business changes you are facing? And, finally, are your people taking the steps required to reinvent their thinking and awareness for the future? Having studied and learnt from these questions you will be well placed to win the knowledge game.

CHAPTER 14

Evaluating your results

'Organisations that don't contribute to society have no right to exist.'—HENRY MINTZBERG

Evaluating your results requires:

- a serious commitment to review
- motivated inquiry and study
- higher standards of business governance
- measuring more than just dollars and economic return
- exploring the real impact of business learning.

Treating measurement as your best friend

There is little point spending hours trying to win the knowledge game if you do not evaluate your efforts. This is a glaring weakness in current business strategy in all industries and countries across the world. The fact is that managers rarely take evaluation seriously and invest time doing it. This observation has been consistently backed up by industry studies for several decades. The American Society for Training and Development again highlighted this conclusion in the *2002 State of the Industry Report,* with only 6 per cent of businesses surveyed evaluating the business impact of their learning and training initiatives (Van Buren and Erskine, 2002). If only managers took a little more time to evaluate and measure the impact of their investment in learning, businesses would be much better placed to capitalise on their strengths as well as address their weaknesses in winning the knowledge game.

The theme of evaluation has been with us as we have travelled through this book. For example, back in Chapter 1 we discussed the importance of each business knowing the gaps between its vision for knowledge and how it actually performs. Then we discussed the importance of review in faster, deeper learning in Chapter 4. In Chapter 6, we noted how by measuring productivity, increasing talent retention and improving levels of customer value, managers will get a better feel for how they are tracking.

Of course the discussions of evaluation and measurement did not end there. In Chapter 10 we introduced the business imperative of calculating and listing your proprietary knowledge and intellectual capital in financial records. Then as we shifted our attention to leveraging digital technology, customer loyalty and e-learning, the importance of critical review and evaluation was also addressed.

Our recurring theme of evaluation should not be a real surprise. Evaluation is about continuous improvement, knowledge enhancement and learning. It has the potential to be a trusted friend, for life, if we only give it a chance. It is the cornerstone of personal and business growth. If we are serious about making a difference and achieving our goals we must review and audit our commitment and success in innovation, learning and knowledge enhancement.

Of course not all measurement and evaluation is good. In fact if we are not careful, what we produce can be inappropriate, meaningless or inaccurate. Just because you are getting great scores, numbers on a balance sheet or you feel good does not necessarily mean you are discovering what you need to know. We have to have a discipline that stretches our boundaries of the known and unknown to reveal the truth.

Excellent evaluation must be backed up with careful planning, transparency and consultation. Management must be prepared to deploy a range of measures without being guilty of producing bad or misleading information. Deploying the right spirit is vitally important. Treat the process of evaluation seriously and you will discover the insights you need to help provide the services and products you desire in a smarter, faster and better way.

To help you get the best out of evaluation of knowledge, learning and innovation, here are five tips to help steer you on the right course:

1. *Avoid measuring everything.* Spend your evaluation efforts on the big projects or mission-critical business processes. Carefully isolate the data and measures that will give you the best and most accurate picture of the truth. This could include performance measures as well as contributing factors such as customer expectations, work environment and the level of management support. Wasting time on trivial matters and squeaky wheels is a serious waste of your resources.

2. *Be wary of accepting benchmarks or standards from other businesses without first studying their suitability and relevance.* Just because someone else has reached a certain standard does not mean it is achievable or relevant in your business. Consider the constraints and idiosyncrasies of your business. Make sure you are clear about what you are trying to do and measure.

3. *Be clear about your real needs and hot spots.* Do your homework before venturing elsewhere to find the answer. Make friends with financial whizzes and industry experts who can help you argue a business case based on facts and the right evidence. Then be prepared to back up your discoveries with testimonials, unsolicited kudos or stories that help build up your picture of success, progress or failure.

4. *Dig below the surface and question assumptions, beliefs and taboos.* Be prepared to ask different questions to map out the next practical step. Your evaluation may tell you how you are going, but it may not tell you what to do next. Ask only those evaluation questions

that you are prepared to answer yourself. Encourage the sharing of important knowledge and unbiased feedback. Be ethical and preserve confidentiality and trust.

5. *Review how well you are conducting the evaluation process itself.* Explore how successful you have been in communicating the intention and purpose of your study or review. Remember the process of measurement must sound both interesting and important, otherwise people will not help you out.

Raising the level of expertise

When a business is evaluating well, it is more likely to discover the value of its wisdom and capability. Each part of a business must be vigilant in discovering new avenues for improved excellence and expertise. Special effort must be made to seek smarter ways of learning and achieving results. Whether it is team learning or studying the merits of a system, the cycle of continuous improvement never stops.

As you would expect, there are many frameworks, methods and formulas that have been produced to help evaluation, measurement and review. However all this assistance is useless, unless people are either motivated or have the time to undertake such an enquiry. So before becoming hooked on the techniques and methods, it is worth asking: Are we serious about doing evaluation? If not, let us talk about why and what can be done. From there you are much better prepared to move forward and take the action required.

For me one of the great revelations that comes from winning the knowledge game is that often worthwhile or interesting discoveries can happen without too much effort at all. Within a few hours of asking a few questions or holding a team discussion you can quickly gather some ideas, intelligence or feedback. It is not as complex as some people would think. If you find people are paralysed by the fear that evaluation is some huge task, break it into small pieces or chunks and enjoy the early success. This will help people to make a start and hopefully see the benefit of evaluation more quickly. It may also unravel any motivation or avoidance problems that may exist.

For example, in preparation for this book, I undertook a brief half-day study to explore what it takes to be a star performer in modern business. Within a few hours of searching the Internet and asking colleagues I found two insights that helped broaden my perspective. Such short bursts of inspiration are the key to winning the knowledge game and helping us grow and enhance our understanding. The first insight was from Jac Fitz-enz and the other was from Rosabeth Moss Kanter. Jac Fitz-enz (2000) in his book *The ROI of Human Capital* shared the findings of the Hay Group's study of a hundred of the most admired companies. He listed what separated the very best from the rest. They found the better performing businesses excelled in a work environment that fostered:

- teamwork
- customer focus
- fair treatment of employees
- initiative and innovation.

The more average performers were more commonly interested in minimising risk, respecting the chain of command, supporting the boss and finally making budget.

Rosabeth Moss Kanter (2001) in her book *Evolve* listed seven qualities that she believed helped shape star performers in world class organisations. They were the proven ability to:

1. display curiosity and imagination that helps people envision and grasp new possibilities
2. make oneself understood by understanding that others have not shared your life experience and as a result they will have a different worldview
3. create bridges of thought and not be confined to a single perspective
4. grasp complexity and make sense out of complicated multipartner relationships
5. care for and feed their teams' bodies and spirit by being sensitive to their needs
6. work with people as resources by respecting what others bring to the table and then listen to their ideas
7. lead through the power of their ideas and strength of their voices rather than any formal position or authority they may hold.

So do not burden people with a process of evaluation and study that digs up resistance and avoidance. Identify key areas for action, make a start and raise the level of expertise. Otherwise serious evaluation will remain in the too hard basket.

Delivering on honesty, transparency and governance

No discussion on measurement or evaluation should be undertaken without addressing the values of honesty and transparency. Without a desire to uncover unbiased and meaningful information and knowledge, it is very hard to achieve lasting success. However unpleasant the results may be, we need to uncover the facts to more forward.

Choosing to play it safe and not share vital insights can lead to unfortunate surprises such as unnecessary losses, damaging downturn or a fall in know-how. This is particularly relevant to the process of business reporting and governance. To overcome the haunting prospects of business failure or destroying of one's reputation, evaluation of one's know-how and performance requires a healthy combination of transparent recording and independent auditing.

To help you maintain a pulse on how serious you treat knowledge as part of your business, here are seven questions to ponder:

1. Does your business see better knowledge and innovation as part of its future?
2. Does your business encourage and reward people for sharing knowledge?
3. Are your systems and processes helping people to collate and disseminate what is being learnt?
4. Does your business protect intellectual property while also nurturing talent?
5. How regularly do you learn from your mistakes, risks and successes?
6. Is the knowledge being gained benefiting your customers, partners and society?
7. What guarantees are there that both evaluation and business governance is transparent, open and truthful?

Whether it is honesty in financial reporting, or the quality of evaluation, there is an increasing expectation that all businesses could perform better. Needless to say the fall out from Enron, WorldCom, HIH, Harris Scarfe, Ansett, Pasminco and One.Tel has added impetus to this cause in recent years. In the US at least 35 per cent of the community did not believe that business was fulfilling its obligations and responsibilities to society (James and Gettler, 2002). There have since been many efforts to raise the standard of reporting and disclosure and management performance.

One such initiative is by the Institute of Social and Ethical AccountAbility, at www.accountability.org.uk. Here businesses are provided with a series of frameworks (i.e. AA1000 and the draft AA2000) to help them improve their accounting, auditing and reporting by being more socially and ethically responsive. A very high value is placed on accuracy and truthfulness, with the aim being the restoration of trust. The specific behaviours that are included in the draft AA2000 framework include:

- developing leading-edge practice in organisational learning and innovation
- creating effective methods for communicating results and progress
- implementing management systems that monitor and learn from business activity, and from the conversations with stakeholders such as employees, customers and the community
- achieving increased public trust, respect and cooperation through transparent reporting and assurance
- creating a governance process that helps to manage risk for optimal performance.

No doubt the benefit of implementing such action has a profound impact on how a business succeeds through knowledge—that is, with the utmost social responsibility, ethical behaviour and integrity. It also provides a catalyst for a cycle of innovation based on partnership with the stakeholders and the community at large. It also increases the chances that what a business reports or claims can be believed.

Businesses that have incorporated these frameworks into their thinking include British Airways, CEMIG (Brazil, power generation), Ford Motor Company, IBM, KPMG, the London International Festival of Theatre, Novo Group (Denmark, health care and industrial enzymes), Tesco and Verizon.

Living on the triple bottom line

In modern business achieving an outstanding profit result is not enough. Society, communities and governments are now expecting an outstanding reputation in other areas as well. A modern business must be a champion on several fronts. Firstly, it must be a consistently high performer in service and product delivery. Secondly, it should be deploying sound and truthful reporting that helps ensure value is being added in both financial and non-financial terms. Then, finally, it should have systems in place that help guarantee it can sustain itself and add value to society.

One such demand is that business be socially and ethically responsible. As was discussed in Chapter 3, managers and their businesses must bypass their ego and the attraction of higher wealth and build a worthwhile purpose. One example is John Huntsman who has built the $US5 billion, 10 000-employee-strong Huntsman Chemical Corporation. Its mission has moved from what could have been labelled a pure profit motive to one quite different. Its current mission includes the following messages: paying off corporate debt, being a responsible corporate citizen and finally relieving human suffering. In recent years the business has been actively involved in many causes which some would argue is not core business. These include donating $US100 million to a cancer centre and building a shelter for homeless in Armenia after an earthquake. John Huntsman argues that this investment has been worth every cent. Not only is such action going to important causes, it also creates a much greater spirit of accomplishment, motivation, unity and teamwork in the business.

Whether it is a small business giving money to a local child-care facility or it is a local artist donating a piece of artwork to a charity, there are many ways we can each make a positive contribution. The goal here is not about being seen to be nice to people; it is about making a worthwhile and positive impact on society, the ecology and the planet. With this focus the impetus for ensuring lasting success takes on a much higher level of importance and intention.

One way of pointing a business on this path is to embrace the triple bottom line. One of the best resources for exploring the triple bottom line on a world scale has been the Global Reporting Initiative (GRI) at www.globalreporting.org. Here intensive collaboration and cooperation between authorities and experts from the UK, India, Canada, Japan, the US and Sweden has produced a range of measures for economic, environmental and social performance.

The result has been a voluntary code on how any business or organisation can take action. The GRI has been very careful in making practical recommendations as to how all businesses can respond in a flexible way and on a voluntary basis. For example, there is a phased incremental implementation for smaller businesses. The simple structure provides an easy-to-maintain process that can be updated and disseminated. The GRI has had a fast uptake with about one hundred companies worldwide taking up the challenge, including Nokia, Procter & Gamble, General Motors, Siemens and South African Breweries. In Australia, as at January 2003, BHP Billiton and City West Water have provided GRI reports voluntarily (Martin, 2003).

Indicators that could be listed under a triple bottom line framework include:

- *economic,* including profitability, productivity, faster research and development, reduced cycle time, high quality decision making, lower training and education costs, agile manufacturing processes, faster customer response, increased rate of innovation and a reduced learning curve
- *environmental,* including the impacts of processes, products and services on air, water, land, biodiversity and human health
- *social,* including workplace health and safety, employee retention, labour rights, child labour, community consultation, morale, and wages and working conditions of staff in all operations.

The idea of the triple bottom line was first introduced to me when studying the pioneering work of the Body Shop. Here is a business that 'walks the talk' in undertaking regular independent reviews of their performance and knowledge in a range of areas, including social and environmental performance and animal protection. For example, did the Body Shop deliver on its core values? Did they meet their goals in the protection of the environment and not harm animals?

This initial discovery led me to uncover many European companies that are spending much more time ensuring a return on investment to customers, employees and trade unions, and not just shareholders. Additionally there is a host of businesses that have used the Kaplan and Norton's (1996) Balanced Scorecard to help improve their capacity to change, reinvent and improve, adopting a more sustainable model for success. Organisations like Harley-Davidson and groups like Business in the Community in the UK (www.bitc.org.uk) and New York Cares (www.nycares.org) have helped forge a better relationship between the business's priorities, social responsibilities and meaningful work. In Australia, a number of retail organisations have signed a 'fair wear' agreement to help protect home-based workers from exploitation. These include: Coles Myer, Country Road, David Jones, Gowings and Big W (Kendall and Manning, 2003).

In the next decade expect to see rapid increases in the area of reporting on the triple bottom line. Already in Northern Europe auditing the triple bottom line is fast becoming an expected business practice. In France, legislation has been introduced so that if a French company wants to be listed on its stock exchange it must make information available to investors on social and environmental performance. In Japan 72 per cent of the country's top 100 companies now produce reports on sustainability. In Australia since March 2002, the *Financial Services Reform Act* requires greater disclosure on labour standards, environmental, social and ethical considerations. Such intervention is leading the surge to greater openness and transparency in business and innovation.

Seven levels of learning evaluation

So far in this chapter we have explored the intention and conduct of evaluation. We will now give some structure to how we can specifically measure the impact and quality of the learning and innovation in a business. So let us explore a model of seven levels of learning evaluation. We begin with the four levels identified by Donald Kirkpatrick (1998), and then a fifth level identified in more recent years by Jack Phillips (2000). Phillips helped move the discussion to a higher plane return on investment (ROI). From there, two more levels are suggested: the sixth is sustainability and the seventh is sharing the benefits. These help lift the exploration of results to include better examination of business governance and the triple bottom line.

Level 1: reaction

Level 1 measures individual reaction to a course or experience. It is the most common form of evaluation used in business, probably because it is perceived as the easiest to do. This form of evaluation is normally seen as an evaluation sheet at the end of a training course. Here we can discover whether a person had a good time and whether it was meaningful. This lowest level of evaluation can raise more questions than answers. For example, just because someone had a wonderful time does not necessarily mean that they learnt something valuable. The reaction method can also be used to evaluate on-the-job coaching and e-learning.

Level 2: learning

At this level attention shifts to what knowledge, skills and attitudes have actually changed or have been acquired during the experience. Commonly changes in learning are determined with some combination of pre- and post-assessment as well as direct observation and testing. Sometimes this evaluation will resolve whether new knowledge or learning had been put to use, but generally the discussion is quite shallow.

Level 3: behaviour

This level measures real change as a result of the initiative being undertaken. This normally involves direct observation of people's performance on the job. For this level of evaluation to be successful requires accurate and unbiased assessment. The assessors are normally the managers, coaches or mentors of the people actually performing the work. To do this well, training and good education on assessment is vital. A skilled assessor will not only note behavioural change, but also which factors may be inhibiting them doing the job in the first place—for example, lack of resources or unclear policy.

Level 4: business results

This level identifies how learning and knowledge is delivered to the business. This would typically involve assessment against measures such as productivity, customer retention, sales and profitability. Depending on the nature of your business, and your interest in knowledge and innovation, this measure will vary. In undertaking this evaluation care must be taken to separate those factors that have nothing to do with the initiative—for example, external pressures such as changed market conditions.

Level 5: return on investment

This level shows the costs versus benefits of an initiative. You will discover the link between learning and improved profitability, efficiency and effectiveness. For example, did the dollar value of the produced benefits exceed the costs of hosting and setting up an initiative? Here some creativity will be required to quantify the hard-to-measure competencies and capabilities. In most cases some measurement can be placed on the data you are receiving; the key is to be clear about the assumptions you are using. There are a number of ratios and measures used; one simple measure recommended by Jack Phillips is return on investment (or ROI):

$$\text{ROI per cent} = \frac{\text{Total benefit (in \$)} \times 100}{\text{Total program cost (in \$)}}$$

Level 6: sustainability

At this sixth level of evaluation we shift our attention to broader and more outward-focused questions. For example, will the knowledge or learning help the business pass the test of time? Here the issue is not just the economics of learning and performance, but also whether the capabilities and competencies being learnt are actually helping a business prepare for the future. We need to pay close attention to the context and environment of change, and be receptive to new views of what excellence means. Typically, businesses that invest in their people and systems, and have a good eye on their environment, will have an increased chance of measuring success. This exploration will help create a better balance of skills in the business, thereby leading to greater agility, longevity and innovation.

Level 7: sharing the benefit

The highest and most altruistic level of evaluation is asking whether your business know-how is adding value and helping others, whether it is your suppliers, customers, partners or society as a whole. As has been highlighted in the discussion on the triple bottom line, business is increasingly expected to be accountable for its actions and be a good corporate citizen, not just for our current generation but for future ones as well. We must be prepared to have independent assessment as well as contribute to the quality of the life of others.

The key to ensuring lasting success is to move up the levels-of-evaluation hierarchy. If you are able to raise questions and stimulate conversations at the higher levels, you will most likely advance over time. Here are some testimonials from people who have been involved in these sorts of discussions in the past:

- 'Customers now feel they are not lost in the system.'
- 'It has enabled peer support and best practice sharing.'
- 'We now view problems from a common perspective.'
- 'We are learning from both our successes and failures.'
- 'We have a much better response to customer needs.'
- 'There is much better communication and openness.'

Summary

Quality evaluation helps shape a stronger future through more honest assessment and deeper thinking about results. To ensure lasting success in business, clear action must be taken to ensure that the generation of value is much broader than just achieving record profits and creating a nice public image. There needs to be independent accountability and verification for social and environmental performance as well. The final mix of evaluation will depend on the nature of your operation and business. Depending on your hot issues and needs, you will use a balance of assessments to achieve the result you desire. If you explore higher levels of evaluation you will soon discover more profound insights, such as greater longevity and shared benefit in what you are doing, while at the lower levels you may only discover what people feel about their learning. The key to success in evaluation is not to burden people with excessive demands but to ensure the right measures are explored for the right reasons. Then your business will be better placed to face the future with confidence.

CHAPTER 15

Measuring your know-how

'You can have all the buildings in the world but it needs people to make the dream a reality.'
—WALT DISNEY

Measuring your know-how requires:

- deeper analysis of how talent generates business value
- creating forward-looking financial statements
- discovering the best measures of knowledge and innovation
- tracking performance over time
- a desire to generate a more enlightened approach.

Meeting the new accounting challenge

There is an increasing realisation that traditional accounting methods fail to measure the real impact of people on the success of a business. On the stock market, there are now many businesses that are valued by many times their financial book value. Twenty years ago when a private sector business valued its wealth, it essentially meant the value of the price equalled the balance-sheet fixed assets, such as buildings, plant and machinery. Now we are seeing a dramatic shift in how worth is being judged. This started with the remarkable case in 1995 of IBM buying Lotus for US$3.5 billion, which was fourteen times the company's book value. The market now places immense value on the value of intangible assets such as intellectual property and know-how. We only have to observe how IBM has benefited from their investment in Lotus to understand how wise their initial decision was.

Oracle provides another example of the value of know-how. Its shareholder value has been worth up to twenty-five times its book value (i.e. 96 per cent for intangible assets and 4 per cent for tangible assets). Such judgments of perceived value indicate that the business community now places a much greater weight on people's ingenuity, talent and imagination. Other examples of the weight given to intangible assets at specific times include Coca-Cola (95 per cent), Kellogg (95 per cent) and interestingly IBM at 93 per cent (www.standardsinstitute.org/background/background3.html; Stewart, 2001).

Even organisations such as Ford, with its massive balance sheet of tangible assets, has a book value of an average 35 per cent of its current market value. The remaining percentage balance is the perceived worth of its know-how. Then there are the many businesses and government operations that are not listed on the stock exchange; their perceived value to customers and the community is often seen to be much more than the cost it takes to run them. People look at the perceived value they contribute to society. A classic example is the host of charities and voluntary organisations that have little or no fixed assets but provide a wonderful service to society.

The measurement of this so-called know-how factor has now become a huge preoccupation for business strategists worldwide. However, there is currently no universal standard or agreement on how this should be done. The Saratoga Institute in the US has developed over 250 measures for what they call human capital. Karl-Erik Sveiby, a pioneer in this field on his website at www.sveiby.com.au, has noted at least twenty-one different approaches to measuring intangible assets or intellectual capital. Given these conflicting opinions and debates on terminology, it is no surprise to discover that accounting for know-how is not yet a normal part of business practice. McKinsey and Company, in a study of thirty-three of Australia's top companies, found that only 25 per cent recognised the importance of intangible-wealth performance, preferring in most cases to see people as a cost rather than wealth generators (www.mckinsey.com.au). However, there is one Swedish Company, Skandia, which has been producing reports on the net worth of their people for nearly a decade.

What makes this field difficult and somewhat controversial is the problem of directly linking knowledge and innovation to better performance. It is difficult to place a monetary value on such factors as high morale, good customer relationships, positive branding and a smart learning culture. We know it is important, but how important is it? For example, when Ford bought Jaguar it reduced the defect rate to 8 per cent of previous levels, but can Ford claim all this success or were there other factors affecting this astounding result?

Another example might be when a business decides to reduce costs by making forced redundancies. On the balance sheet such cost cutting may give a favourable result, but what about the loss of talent, fall in morale and reduced customer loyalty? Will the decision have a direct or indirect impact on the long-term capability and viability of the business? Such questions are central to modern management's desire to ensure lasting success through better reporting of the value of its knowledge.

Finding common ground

There are now many accounting bodies and industry groups researching how intangible assets can be better recorded. This is leading to a profound shift in thinking in how to undertake annual reviews and forecasts. It was not long ago that using measures or indicators such as brands, customer lists and technology were seen as unthinkable. However, in the world of the digital-age company, such accounting and business reporting is becoming a necessity. In the next decade the reporting of so-called intangible assets will dramatically change the accounting landscape. For the first time investors and the public will have a greater opportunity to place a better measure on the true value and future of an enterprise. It will also provide internal decision makers with data to improve cycles of knowledge and innovation.

We can already see this with Coca-Cola, whose brand equity and protection of its secret formula is valued in the billions; or Merck who with clever investment in research and development is able to use their acquired insight to help grow competitive advantage. In the world of entertainment, the Sydney Opera House through their website at www.sydneyoperahouse.com smartly markets their intellectual property to improve customer loyalty and market share.

Of course saying that intangible assets should be recorded is one thing, but reaching agreement on how to do it is another. To help address this, the International Accounting Standards Board is working hard to release some much-needed guidelines for implementation in 2005 (Day, 2003). You may wish to visit www.iasb.org.uk for the latest information on this. Already the Financial Accounting Standards Board (FASB) in the US has said that measures of intangible values must be:

- selected very carefully
- displayed in a systematic and ordered way using matrixes or tables
- used across a business or organisation rather than in isolation
- compared between periods of time and with other relevant organisations, divisions or industries
- supported with explanatory notes to guide the reader through the material (e.g. where old measures are no longer used and new ones brought in, this should be explained).

The great dilemma for many experts is that placing value on talent and genius is seen as a very imprecise science, and many of the measures and indicators are seen as unreliable. However, in saying this, relying on traditional financial reporting only is even more dangerous—particularly if we consider investments in our people, training, innovation, and research and development are currently treated as costs within existing accounting methods.

As Wayne Upton Jr wrote in conjunction with Edmund Jenkins (2001), businesses should be required produce reports that demonstrate:

- a recognition of intangible assets in financial statements and improved measures of those assets
- an expanded and systematic use of non-financial performance metrics
- an increased use of forward-looking information.

In noting the need for change, most accounting professionals and many industry observers are very cautious and not likely to suggest massive change overnight. Businesses cannot throw out mandatory financial records and then duplicate this with another set of books that are unrealistic, unnecessary and unlawful. So expect a phased and incremental introduction rather than a revolution.

It must also be said that many managers are very hesitant about disclosing information to the public that could be used against them in the future. Others, however, will be very keen to share their story of how they are growing expertise, talent and know-how. As former chairperson of Lend Lease Corporation Stuart Hornery said at a Symposium on Measuring and Reporting Intellectual Capital: 'measuring intangible assets should be voluntary and should report on the matters that matter most to performance'.

When it comes to reporting intangible assets it is imperative these disclosures are true and accurate. We hardly want another set of reports that have questionable integrity. As with traditional measurements of tangible assets, any measures of intangible value must be relevant, reliable, clear and verifiable, and provide a consistent basis of comparison from period to period.

Exploring sources of knowledge and innovation

When it comes to measuring know-how, no one approach can meet all needs. Specific measures or indicators are heavily influenced by the nature of the operations that exist within each business. For example, a marketing function could use measures like the annual loss of key accounts or churn rate as a measure of the worth of their know-how. A human resource function could disclose staff turnover as a measure. An operations function could see investment in research and development and a list of major clients as far more meaningful. Again these measures will vary enormously between profit-driven and not-for-profit enterprises and are highly idiosyncratic. Therefore it is imperative that assumptions that drive business reporting are communicated loud and clear. In some cases managers may be immediately attracted to a measure of knowledge and innovation, while on other occasions they will need to shop around.

There are indicators for private sector accounts that can supplement the more traditional measures, such as profitability, productivity, goodwill and increased sales growth. In government, measures could include productivity gains, capital outlays and savings to help provide a picture of success in innovation and knowledge. However, such blanket measures at best only give a quick impression. It is therefore recommended that a series of measures be considered in helping promote a more accurate and informative picture of your business landscape. Here are five areas commonly explored in existing reporting on intangible value:

1. *Customer capital* attempts to place a value on the nature and quality of customer relationships, customer satisfaction rates, growth of customer learning, involvement and improvement in decision making and consultation.

2. *Human capital* measures the current know-how of people under the business's control. Jac Fitz-enz describes human capital as 'that intellectual asset that goes home every night in the minds of employees'. He also argues that it is the only capital that is active. Without it, organisations cannot function. A high level of enthusiasm, desire and commitment in the workplace would be an indicator that the human capital or available talent is working in your favour in a business.

3. *Intellectual capital* constitutes listings and perceived values of trademarks, trade secrets, patents and branding.

4. *Relationship capital* involves describing important strategic alliances, collaborative relationships, business partnerships, joint ventures and industry associations, which could help build reputation and industry standing.

5. *Systems performance* explores how systems and processes directly or indirectly benefit or generate improved know-how. Measures can include the investment in digital technology or how practices have been replicated or improved. Here you might find measures of productivity, reduced wastage and efficiency savings.

Selecting your best measures

To assist in the use of suitable measures of intangible value, listed below are examples of metrics that commonly appear in reports. This list is general in nature and is not all-inclusive. It is designed to give you a sense of the area and give you a chance to explore options. Like me you will find it fascinating to see the degree of inconsistency across industries, not only between businesses but also and, more alarmingly, between divisions or work locations within an operation. The aim is to promote conversations in your business on how you could better place the value of your know-how and enhance the power of your knowledge. This listing of intangible asset measures comes from a variety of sources, including work by the US Financial Accounting Standards Board, the International Accounting Standards Board, R. S. Kaplan and D. P. Norton (2001a), Karl-Erik Sveiby (1997), Jac Fitz-enz (2000), the Saratoga Institute, Skandia AF and the Danish Agency for the Development of Trade and Industry.

Examples of intangible asset measures

Customer capital

- agreements, contracts and permits
- average response rate to customers
- customer acquisition cost
- customer churn rates
- customer satisfaction
- customer yield
- listings and numbers of customers
- market share
- on-line sales per day
- ratio of sales contacts to sales closed
- revenue percentage per customer
- repeat orders
- service awards
- share of new customers

Human capital

- average years of service
- brain-drain rate and cost of voluntary separations as a percentage of head count
- employee satisfaction (e.g. per cent of employees scoring in top quartile of job satisfaction survey)
- expert turnover
- hiring cost
- hours and dollar investment of training/employees
- level and type of education
- literacy levels (e.g. per cent of key employees who have met competency standards)
- number of employees
- profitability per employee
- proportion of support staff to the core business
- rookie ratio
- staff morale (e.g. per cent of employees who indicate concerns with existing culture and climate)
- staff turnover
- success of employee suggestion programs
- succession planning (e.g. per cent of key positions with at least one fully qualified person ready)

Intellectual capital

- brand names
- computer software and licences
- industry awards
- Internet domain names
- patents, copyrights, franchises, trademarks (i.e. perceived value)
- patents cited by others
- rights (e.g. broadcasting or servicing agreements)
- unpatented technology (e.g. secret formulas)

Relationship capital

- business partnerships
- contract portfolio
- cross-functional teamwork (e.g. per cent of projects based on interdisciplinary collaboration)

- joint ventures
- knowledge-enhancing customers and suppliers
- projects being undertaken with others (e.g. colleagues, customers and idea groups)
- strategic alliances

Systems performance

- administrative expenses as a percentage of sales
- break-even time for new product or service development
- cash flow
- cycle times to process services or products
- investment in information technology or knowledge management systems
- knowledge-reuse hits from learning archives or databases
- new product introductions
- on-time delivery
- productivity gains due to new ideas or equipment
- quarterly sales growth
- research and development expenditure and per cent directly involved
- sales generated from new products and services
- time to completion of new products
- unit cost of manufacture or service delivery

Clearing the fog

Without a doubt the area of measuring know-how is undergoing fundamental change. For some the pace of reform is too slow, while for others it is a very scary proposition. This has led to an intense debate on the perceived and actual value of specific measures.

I recently attended a talk on this topic and the conversation became very heated. One area of contention was how to place a value on the notion of a corporate or business culture. For the presenter, who was an accountant, he argued that business culture was not an asset; it cannot be controlled and owned. So placing a value on its perceived worth was meaningless. Yet others in the audience took another view. They argued that the attitudes of staff and how they feel towards the business and its customers must be reported on. They argued that a so-called bad culture has a debilitating effect on knowledge and innovation in any business or team. In that situation everything in a business becomes difficult. Not surprisingly, they felt efforts must be taken to measure the culture of a business.

Clearing the fog surrounding measuring know-how does not stop there. For example, what is the benefit of putting a dollar value on an invention if the person who was primarily involved in its development leaves the organisation? (This is especially so if a business has not captured the individual's insights and knowledge before they left.) As you can see, clearing the fog is not an easy task and it can raise more questions than it answers. However, it is time for managers to search for and trial different measures. As long as it is done in an accurate and truthful way, business will benefit, particularly if accountability is high and the business looks to generate a more enlightened approach.

So sit back and watch as the debate on placing a better value on knowledge and innovation is explored in the decade ahead. This topic will be firmly on the agenda for many years to come. However, in saying that, managers cannot afford to wait to deploy a range of measures that go beyond just reporting tangible assets. We need to mine out what knowledge is vital and why, then stimulate methods, tools and systems to make it easier to succeed. We may not be able to totally clear the fog, but we can improve the level of awareness and inquiry on how know-how adds value.

Summary

In the knowledge era businesses can no longer measure performance and potential purely on traditional financial reports that focus on tangible assets. What is required is a fresh approach to exploring how knowledge—or intangible assets—fuels business success. It is vital that each business explores how its know-how is creating value. For example, what is the current standing in how the business relates to its customers? How successful is the business in stimulating a healthy learning culture while protecting its intellectual property? Is the business able to build the systems and processes it needs to foster improved innovation and service delivery? Such questions are central to ensuring lasting success. Only when such conversations and reporting become second nature will there be a formula for long-term growth, renewal and inspiration.

CHAPTER 16

Passing the final test

'The dynamic principle of fantasy at play, which belongs to the child, appears to be inconsistent with the principles of serious work. But without this playing with fantasy, no creative work has ever yet come to birth.'—CARL JUNG

Passing the final test requires:

- being a magnet for learning in everyday life
- questioning our self-talk and inner dialogue
- removing our ego from the equation
- being aware of our arrogance and overconfidence
- rediscovering the spirit of play at work.

Coming back to basics

At the beginning of Chapter 1, we started with two vital questions:

1. What makes a truly outstanding business?
2. What capabilities does a business generate that makes it extra-ordinary and very hard to copy?

Over the last fifteen chapters there have been many suggestions made to help in your ability to answer these questions. Whatever your reflections and feelings, your journey will need to continue. When we stop asking these questions it is likely that we have lost the focus we need to run a successful business or build a better career. So place them firmly on the agenda and use them as a reference point to position and increase the power of your knowledge.

If we were to take a poll on the major theme of this book, my sense is that many basic ideas would come to mind. Here are seven that were in my thoughts as I wrote this book:

*   collaboration
*   a compelling vision
*   digital technology
*   deeper learning
*   flow
*   a safe space
*   review.

Of course depending on your needs and experience there may be many other themes that jumped out for you. I am most interested in hearing about and discussing your thoughts and conclusions. I would strongly encourage you to contact me at www.alastairrylatt.com and share your ideas with me. I will do my best to reply within a few days.

As we reach the final pages it is imperative that we again remind ourselves of some key messages. Firstly, if we wish to win the knowledge game we must have a very clear reason for our learning. We need to understand why we are bothering to develop our capabilities, while also understanding who else will stand to benefit. Our dreams, goals and intentions are drivers that maintain our curiosity and passion. Whether it is establishing learning goals or mapping out a plan for a business, such focus can never be undervalued. It is the impetus that guides and motivates us.

Having explored their focus and motivation, managers can then shift their attention to improving systems, programs and processes. In business this means championing practical ways for people to exchange, store and share vital insight and innovation. For this to happen there must be simple and clearly understood ways for people to contribute and innovate. With this attitude a business will be off to a flying start, not because it can control and package the knowledge generated but because it will be feeding and nurturing a learning process that is resilient, adaptive and enduring.

Remember, be a magnet for learning. Radiate your brilliance not by showing how much you know but by creating a climate for others to show their genius. Secure lasting success by creating openness, receptivity and a curious nature. Foster a spirit that sees wisdom in various people, places and forms, while allowing others to do the same. Nurture the learning that you have at your disposal. Know when to enlighten and stimulate, but also when to give ample space and opportunity to grow. Be aware of those people who stifle learning and knowledge and remind them of their responsibilities, while clearly understanding why they see the world as they do. Then work towards building a shared commitment to a better and exciting future.

Like in any game, success rarely happens overnight; you need to be in it for the long haul. If you reach a hurdle or are confused, avoid becoming paralysed. See the creative tension as a new opportunity to share ideas and build better understanding. Be prepared to review your plans and vision and make modifications. Breaking new ground is rarely done in a zone of familiarity and comfort. Quantum leaps in learning most often occur when we are forced or choose to do something new or different, which leads to new behaviours, assumptions and mental models.

Of course winning the knowledge game cannot be sustained in an atmosphere of fear and compliance. Managers need to inspire confidence, learn from mistakes and celebrate success. We also need to be grateful for our strengths and the gifts we bring, as well as having a healthy approach to self-improvement and growth.

From experience, being able to work and learn together is far more important than any financial, technical or technological solution. We need to connect emotionally, intellectually and spiritually if we are to grow and succeed. Businesses and more specifically managers are notoriously bad at managing relationships. It is very easy to have a healthy relationship when things are rosy and times are good, but it is when things take a turn for the worse that the real test begins.

In business as in life, relationship skills should never be assumed; they must be developed and worked on. It is not so much that people do not have the technical skills, it is that they do not have the desire or the ability to get on with each other. People need to discuss more rigorously how they can work better together by building a shared and worthwhile purpose. All too often a business's visions and plans fail to connect with the values and hopes of its people. If only a little more time were spent on forming relationships, the potential for teamwork, shared commitment and learning would be so much greater. No level of business acumen will help you if you are unable to generate trust and mutual advantage.

Listening to our instincts

Life's challenges constantly stoke up a fire of emotions and thoughts. At times we feel in control and happy, while at other times we might feel quite vulnerable, alone or angry. How we respond to our state of mind and how we process our own inner thoughts is where the knowledge game is eventually won or lost. In saying this, I am not suggesting you undertake some mind control training or you run off and see a psychiatrist, but I am suggesting that you develop the skill to tune into your mind and instincts more. Our job is not to fight a war against the gods and monsters of the mind, but to take more liberties in how we can learn and respond to what our minds might be saying.

For me, it is here that the final test of winning the knowledge game needs to be undertaken and understood. We need to cast away those rogue thoughts and delusions that are causing us harm, even when on the surface the intentions may be very positive and enticing. Similarly we need to recognise the power of our intuition and gut feeling. At times our instinct is wrong, but more often than not our inner wisdom is right or we discover a hidden issue that needs exploring.

Listening to our instincts requires us to understand that our minds are a blending of both conscious and subconscious activity. Scientific research has shown that we have a complex array of different neurological, hormonal and electromagnetic information. Each moment of time we are trying to make meaning and interpret what is going on around us. Sometimes we may check into our inner dialogue or self-talk to help us, but most of the time our mind is clearly making decisions without consulting us.

As neuropsychologist Richard Gregory explains, most of our mental functioning is done without us ever being aware of it. He gives the following analogy (Restak, 2000):

> Imagine consciousness as a beam of light, from a torch directed around the dark universe of the mind. We are the beam of light; we are an eye looking along the beam, and we see nothing outside. But there is a great deal around it and much that is never illuminated. All this is Mind. Present consciousness is what we see lit by the patch of light of the beam.

Further studies by Professor Benjamin Libet and Dr Patrick Haggard have found that our subconscious always starts with a whole series of electrical activity before we respond or act consciously (Greenfield, 2001). On average this takes between one-half to one-quarter of a second to process.

So in a real sense we are always living in the past and a great deal of our thinking, emotional juggling and judgments are made before we even get the urge to do something. All this mental activity in our mind is our personal attempt to deal with complexity and this helps us to think in a single and coherent whole. So we should not see our conscious thinking and feeling as our whole mind; clearly it is not.

Professor Michael Gazzaniga (2002) proposes that we sometimes label our conscious mind or inner voice as being only from the left side of our brain. This left side of our brain tries to make meaning and explanation from the various events and emotions we are experiencing. In fact the left side of the brain looks for order and reason even when none exists. This leads to overgeneralisation, mistakes and errors.

As Gazzaniga explains, the left side of our brain sings like Pavarotti while the right is like a bird chirping in the background. He goes on to say that the feeling of being in control of our lives is just an illusion. The urge to do something does not come from conscious thought but starts with the electrical energy between the billions of neurons and pathways in our subconscious mind. The vast majority of what we are doing is never in our awareness. In fact if you try to be aware of what you are doing you will fail. Your conscious mind does not have a hope of managing the complexity of such an activity. It is all being done for us without us thinking about it. Try the next time you are walking down the street to manage the complexity of what you are doing. For people who have had to learn to walk again after an accident or illness, using conscious thought to walk is a difficult task.

Given these findings, it is not surprising that people have for thousands of years sought better ways to increase the awareness of their mind. Such an enquiry is vital if we want to address the problems and complexities of life and find different connections and choices. The same message applies to business. We can never hope to make total sense of our know-how as it often lies hidden and out of reach. The best we can do is create a spirit of learning, which encourages risk taking, deeper thinking and experimentation. Then, whatever happens to us in business, we have an attitude that will carry us through.

Dealing with our ego

Each of us has an ego—a part of our psyche that desperately wants to help us. We probably cannot go an hour without our ego making judgments for us—whether it is accepting praise or choosing to tune out when we are in danger of hearing something that may upset us.

Recently, I had to give a talk on the topic of 'ego-less leadership'. For the two weeks leading up to this talk, I noticed how my ego was affecting my life. It was a fascinating experience and I must say it changed me forever. I discovered how quickly my ego hijacked my learning and thinking even when it was not in my best interests to do so. In doing my research I came across a quote from Alan Watts, which helped shape my thinking for this presentation. He said way back in 1966 in *The Book On The Taboo Against Knowing Who You Are* that we have created a false illusion of a human being and are aware of ourselves as only ego inside 'bags of skin'.

The problem with an ego is that it can stop us from discovering important lessons in life. For example, we may choose to be hurt when someone confronts our point of view or questions what we are doing. Often our natural response is to become defensive and to not hear the feedback. This personalisation also extends to good news when we can gloat over what nice things are being said about us. The real test occurs when we remove ourselves from the equation and discover the important lessons that lie behind the feedback we are receiving.

I noticed this again when I attended a training session by an expert in knowledge management. Although the content was marvellous, it was obvious that many of the participants had some difficulty coming to terms with the material. Instead of using the resistance as an opportunity to learn more, the presenter chose to bulldoze on and present his material regardless. During the lunch break when I brought this to his attention, his ego took over and he disregarded my feedback. He clearly wanted to be seen as an expert and as the holder of all wisdom and was not prepared to compromise his approach. Then as the training session progressed into the afternoon, a clear polarisation of learners began to surface. Some people of course felt OK about the style and delivery, while others felt quite alienated and frustrated. The real shame was that the ego of the presenter had got in the way; had he demonstrated greater flexibility the outcome from the training course would have been a lot better for more people.

This story leads to the second point about our ego: ego can paralyse our thinking and we can become attached to an idea, opinion or outcome. If our view is questioned or attacked we can choose to be hostile or feel wounded. Again such blocking and filtering does not help us to grow. We need to allow ourselves the freedom to hear and discuss a diverse range of opinions and not let our ego take a premature exit from what is being discussed.

We commonly see how ego wants to win out when people fall into the trap of 'if only' thinking. For example, 'if only' this person would agree with me, or 'if only' someone understood. Such craving or attachment is directly related to our ego's desire to control. We often see this when managers try to lead or coach their staff, resulting in a style that is more about telling and compliance than exploring different avenues and viewpoints. The sad consequence is often an impasse where nobody wins or progresses.

In business a common cause of failure is arrogance. People can fall into the trap of being too confident about their ability or too caught up in their success. This includes an attitude of invincibility leading to a serious loss of rapport with customers, staff and the marketplace. This ego-driven arrogance has enormous repercussions in winning the knowledge game and business success. If you feel you know everything it is very difficult to make progress. As John Matthews, a consultant in executive coaching, reminded me recently, 'if someone is sleeping you can wake them up, but if they are pretending to sleep you will never wake them up'.

So what can you do about arrogance? As a general principle we must always seek to improve, irrespective of how well we feel we are going. It is only then that we will have the openness of mind to discover new perspective and learn from our mistakes. To help avoid arrogance, consider the following five suggestions:

1. Hold a six monthly review of your strengths, weaknesses, opportunities and threats.
2. Assume your competition is clever and competent.
3. Listen and take action based on regular consultation with customers and key partners such as staff, managers and trade unions.
4. Undertake regular industry visits and attend conferences to discover new insights.
5. Read widely and learn broadly.

Of course our ego is only half the equation. We have to adapt to other people's ego as well. We must understand where our ego is a factor as well as the other person's. We need to have trust and faith in the process of listening and sharing knowledge. This personal commitment to two-way rapport is essential if we are to be successful in passing the final test of winning the knowledge game.

Here are seven tips to help you get past the hidden tiger of ego:

1. Rapport is everything. Get to know the other person's story and needs first.
2. Paraphrase not only what the other person is saying but also how they might be feeling and thinking.
3. Confirm common ground and areas of acceptance. Issues are rarely black and white, so be prepared to be surprised.
4. Offer to help the other person by providing better information, resources or tools.
5. Use neutral language without laying blame. Give feedback without upsetting or overly gratifying the ego.

6. Clarify your views and feelings. Ask the other person to repeat back what you have said and how you might be feeling.
7. Always thank the other person for them granting you the opportunity to have the conversation.

Living a simple game plan

Winning the knowledge game is a major challenge in modern business. One could reasonably argue that it has always been our challenge. However the twenty-first century world of the super highway and the knowledge worker places enormous pressure and expectations on us all. I would liken the challenge of trying to keep up to date in this field to pouring sand over your outstretched hand. Sometimes you may be lucky, and some of the wisdom will stick, but often it just falls away. The key is to live a game plan that enables you to deal with such volumes and complexity and achieve a good outcome.

Three practical questions have helped me on this journey and may help you:

1. Who am I?
2. What do I stand for?
3. Where am I going?

In business you may ask something like:

1. What is our mission?
2. What do we stand for?
3. Where are we going?

For me these questions provide the glue to achieving greater meaning and purpose in life, as well as helping achieve excellence and success in business. This is not because these questions are especially clever or new, but because they give us the chance to shape our dreams and to be an active participant in achieving our goals in whatever form they might take.

Winning the knowledge game is something that goes beyond learning the latest, the best or achieving the next target. It is our way of rediscovering the spirit we need to maintain the fun in our lives, whether it is at home or at work. Take every opportunity to explore the wonder of learning, whether reading a new book, playing in the park or tasting new food. Love what you do and be prepared to find new ways of looking at the world. Question the so-called truth, go out and test your assumptions and question your intuition. Be prepared to try the untested, the unknown and discover more. Turn off the television, engage your senses, take on new challenges, stretch your comfort zone and reclaim what it means to be you.

Summary

The ultimate skill in winning the knowledge game is in building a clear and uncluttered mind that is more receptive to the moments we face. To do this we need to realise that our conscious thoughts are only a fraction of our mind's activity and we are really at the mercy of our subconscious. By beginning a regular daily practice of noticing our self-talk and ego, we are well on the way to a path of greater personal growth and development. It is here where the knowledge game needs to be won for us to succeed. If we can explore how our mind works and how it impacts on our view of the world, we are wonderfully placed to achieve lasting success in whatever we choose to do.

References

Alfredson, K. (2001), 'Accounting for identifiable intangibles—An unfinished standard-setting task', *Australian Accounting Review*, 12, 2, July, pp. 12–38.

Arnott, G. (2002), 'Hitting the small screen', *Marketing and eBusiness*, July, pp. 12–18.

Australian Accounting Review (2001), 'Accounting for intangibles', *Australian Accounting Review*, 12, 2, July, pp. 2–3.

Australian Institute of Management (2002), 'Agenda-knowledge Management', *Management Today*, Australian Institute of Management, Sydney, July.

Australian Institute of Training and Development (2002), *E-learning Special Report*, Australian Institute of Training and Development, Sydney.

Australian Medical Association (2001), 'Sphere: A national depression project', *The Medical Journal of Australia*, 175, 16 July.

Bagshaw, M. & Phillips, P. (2000), *Knowledge Management*, Fenman, Cambridgeshire, UK.

Barnett, R. C. & Hall, D. T. (2001), 'How to use reduced hours to win the war for talent', *Organizational Dynamics*, Winter, pp. 192–209.

Barrett, R. (1998), *Liberating the Corporate Soul: Building a visionary organization*, Reed Educational and Professional Publishing, Melbourne.

Baum, G., Ittner, C., Larcker, D., Low, J., Siefeld, T. & Malone, M. (2000), 'Introducing the new value creation index', *Forbes ASAP*, 45, 7, at www.forbes.com/asap/1000/0403/140.html.

Benoussan, B. (1998), 'Why spy? Using competitive intelligence to boost your business', *Management*, pp. 56–8.

Bergeron, B. (2001), *The Eternal E-customer*, McGraw-Hill, New York.

Berry, M. & Linoff, G. (2000), *Mastering Data Mining*, John Wiley & Sons, New York.

Bonabeau, E. & Meyer, C. (2001), 'Swarming intelligence: A whole new way to think about business', *Harvard Business Review*, May, pp. 107–14.

Boone, M. (2001), *Managing Inter@ctively*, McGraw-Hill, New York.

Botkin, J. (1999), *Smart Business: How knowledge communities can revolutionize your company*, Free Press, New York.

Brinkerhoff, R. (2000), 'Use evaluation as a strategic tool to build performance improvement capability', *Training and Development in Australia*, August, pp. 14–20.

Brown, J. S. & Duguid, P. (2000), 'Balancing act: How to capture knowledge without killing it', *Harvard Business Review*, May–June, pp. 73–80.

Bukowitz, W. & Williams, R. L. (1999), *The Knowledge Management Fieldbook*, Financial Times Prentice Hall, London.

Business Council of Australia (2001), *Towards Sustainable Development*, Business Council of Australia, Melbourne.

Cacioppe, R. (2000), 'Creating spirit at work: Re-visioning organization development and leadership', *The Leadership & Organization Development Journal*, 1, 21, 1, pp. 48–54, and 2, 21, 1 and 2, pp. 110–19.

Cameron, F. (2003), 'Sales force', *HR Monthly*, February, pp. 20–5.

Chapnick, S. (2001), 'Scotland does e-learning', *T + D*, August, pp. 42–53.

Clutterbuck, D. (2000), 'Ten core mentor competencies' *Organizations and People*, 7, 4, November, pp. 29–34.

Con'e, J. W. & Robinson, D. G. (2001), 'The power of e-performance', *T + D*, August, pp. 32–41.

Czechowicz, J. (2001), 'You can't choose your family, but you can choose your customers', *Management Today*, November–December, pp. 10–11.

Da Silva, A. & L'Estrange, A. (2001), 'How to handle workplace bullies', *Human Resources*, December, pp. 21–4.

Danish Trade and Industry Development Council (1997), *Intellectual Capital Accounts Reporting and Managing Intellectual Capital*, Danish Trade and Industry Development Council, Copenhagen.

Day, P. (2003), 'Countdown 2005', *CFO*, February, pp. 30–40.

De Geus, A. (1997), *The Living Company*, Nicholas Brealey Publishing, London.

De Long, D. & Seeman, P. (2000), 'Confronting conceptual confusion and conflict in knowledge management', *Organizational Dynamics*, Summer, pp. 33–43.

Davenport, T. & Beck, J. (2001), *The Attention Economy*, Harvard Business School Press, Boston.

Davenport, T. H. & Prusak, L. (1998), *Working Knowledge: How organizations manage what they know*, Harvard Business School Press, Boston.

Dearlove, D. (2001), 'Finding the CEO within', *Silverkris*, June, pp. 26–8.

Denning, S. (2000), *The Springboard: How storytelling ignites action in knowledge-era organisations*, Butterworth Heinemann, London.

Dess, G. G. & Picken J. C. (2000), 'Changing roles: Leadership in the 21st century', *Organizational Dynamics*, Winter, pp. 18–33.

Dick, B. (1987), *Helping Groups To Be Effective*, Interchange Publishers, Brisbane.

Dick, B. & Dalmau, T. (1999), *Values in Action,* 2nd edn, Interchange Publishers, Brisbane.

Dixon, N. (2000), *Common Knowledge,* Harvard Business School Press, Boston.

Downes, L. & Mui, C. (1998), *Killer Applications: Digital strategies for market dominance*, Harvard Business School Press, Boston.

Drake Business Review (2002), 'How knowledge-based enterprises really get built: A conversation with Dr Jac Fitz-enz', *Drake Business Review*, 1, Drake International, Melbourne.

Dutka, A. (1999), *Competitive Intelligence for the Competitive Edge*, American Marketing Association, NTC Business Books, New York.

e-commerce today (2000), 'It's the end of the office as we know it', *e-commerce today*, August, pp. 6–8.

Evans, T. (2001), 'Wave riders', *HR Monthly*, October, pp. 14–17.

Eysenck, H. (1988), 'Personality, stress and cancer: Prediction and prophylaxis', *British Journal of Medical Psychology*, pp. 57–75.

Fisher, S. (2001), 'On-line learning', *Training and Development in Australia*, April, pp. 8–9.

Fitz-enz, J. (2000), *The ROI of Human Capital*, AMACOM, New York.

Fitzgerald, A. (1998), *Intellectual Property,* LBC Information Services, Sydney.

Garnaut, J. (2002), 'Part-timers want more work, but can't find it', *Sydney Morning Herald,* November.

Gazzaniga, M. (2002), 'The split brain revisited', 'The hidden mind—special edition', *Scientific American*, 12, 1, pp. 26–31.

Global Reporting Initiative (2000), 'Sustainability reporting guidelines on economic, environmental and social performance', Global Reporting Initiative, Boston.

Goffee, R. & Jones, G. (2000), 'Why should anyone be led by you?' *Harvard Business Review*, September–October, pp. 63–70.

Goleman, D. (1998), *Working With Emotional Intelligence*, Bloomsbury, London.

Gray, S. (2002), 'Knowledge the key to survival: Crowther', *Brisbane Chronicle*, 25 May, p. 17.

Greenfield, S. (2001), *Brain Story: Unlocking our inner world of emotions, memories, ideas and desires*, BBC Worldwide Ltd.

Greenwich, C. (1997), *The Fun Factor*, McGraw-Hill, Sydney.

Gummesson, E. (1999), *Total Relationship Marketing*, Butterworth Heinemann, Oxford.

Ham, P. (2001), 'B2B is the key', *Your Business,* May–June, pp. 12–15.

Harkins, J. P., Carter, L. & Timmins, A. (2000), *Best Practices in Knowledge Management and Organizational Learning Handbook,* Linkage Inc., Lexington, Massachusetts.

Harry, M. & Schroder, R. (2000), *The Six Sigma: The breakthrough management strategy revolutionizing the world's top companies*, Currency, New York.

Herrmann, N. (1996), *The Whole Brain Business Book,* McGraw-Hill, New York.

Hockley, A. (2001), 'Beware of storks', *Marketing and eBusiness*, April, pp. 46–9.

Horin, A. & Wilson, V. (2001), 'A nation of work, stress and no play', *Sydney Morning Herald*, 5 September, p. 3.

Houghton, M. (2002), 'The sins of CRM', *Marketing and eBusiness*, July, pp. 22–6.

Hsien Lim, L. (2001), 'Protecting your intellectual property', *Straits Times*, 4 April, p. 22.

Hubbard, G. Samuel, D., Heap, S. & Cocks, G. (2002), *The First XI: Winning organisations in Australia*, John Wiley & Sons, Brisbane.

Human Resources (2001), 'E-learning: Teaching meets technology', *Human Resources*, November, pp. 22–4.

Human Resources Magazine (2001), 'Knowledge management: Taming the information beast', *Human Resources Magazine*, 11–1, pp. 15–17.

Hunter, V. (1997), *Business to Business Marketing*, McGraw-Hill, New York.

Institute of Social and Ethical AccountAbility (1999), *AccountAbility 1000—AA1000 Overview*, AccountAbility, London.

—— (2001), *AA2000, AccountAbility Management—Consultation Briefing 1*, AccountAbility, London.

IP Australia (2000), *Intellectual Property: IP—Don't give away your most valuable asset*, IP Australia, Canberra, May.

James, D. & Gettler, L. (2002), 'Recovering a lost reputation', *Management Today*, November–December, pp. 14–19.

Jenkins, E. & Upton, W. (2001), 'Internally generated intangible assets: Framing the discussion', *Australian Accounting Review*, 12, 2, July, pp. 4–11.

Kanter, R. M. (2001), *Evolve*, Harvard Business School Press, Boston.

Kaplan, R. S. & Norton, D. P. (1996), *The Balanced Scorecard*, Harvard Business School Press, Boston.

—— (2001a), 'Leading change with the Balanced Scorecard', *Financial Executive*, 17, 6, Spring, pp. 64–6.

—— (2001b), 'Transforming the Balanced Scorecard from performance management to strategic management: Part 1', *Accounting Horizons*, 15, March, pp. 87–104.

Karwat, A. (2001), 'What you don't know can hurt you', *Management Today,* May, pp. 6–7.

Kaufman, R. (2000), *Mega-planning*, Sage Publications, Thousand Oaks, California.

Kaye, B. & Jordon-Evans, S. (1999), *Love 'Em or Lose 'Em*, Berrett-Koehler, San Francisco.

—— (2002), 'Retention in tough times', *T + D*, American Society for Training and Development, January, pp. 32–7.

Kendall, R. & Manning, P. (2003), 'The good, the bad and the ugly', *Ethical Investor*, 19, February, pp. 18–21.

Kirkpatrick, D. (1998), *Evaluating Training Programs*, 2nd edn, Berrett-Koehler, San Francisco.

James, D. (2001), 'Knowledge in action', *Business Review Weekly*, 23 February, pp. 75–8.

Langford, P. (2002), 'The value and loyalty matrix', *Management Today*, January–February, p. 40.

Leonard, D. (1998), *Wellsprings of Knowledge,* Harvard Business School Press, Boston.

Levinson, J. C. (1998), *Guerrilla Marketing,* 3rd edn, Houghton Mifflin, Boston.

Long, D. D. & Seemann, P. (2000), 'Confronting conceptual confusion and conflict in knowledge management', *Organizational Dynamics*, Summer, pp. 33–43.

Long, S. & Yeo, A. (2001), 'Plane names and simple trust keep staff happy', *The Straits Times*, 6 September, p. H2.

Lubit, R. (2001), 'Tacit knowledge and knowledge management: The keys to sustainable competitive advantage', *Organizational Dynamics*, Winter, pp. 165–78.

McCraty, K. (2001), *Science of the Heart*, HeartMath Research Center, Institute of HeartMath, Boulder Creek, California.

Macken, J. (2002), 'Trick or treat', *Boss Magazine*, October, pp. 36–9.

Marketing and ebusiness (2001a), 'Robot kills call centre staff', *Marketing and ebusiness*, November.

—— (2001b), 'Buyer beware', *Marketing and ebusiness*, December, p. 4.

Marquardt, M. (1999), *Action Learning in Action*, Davies-Black Publishing, Palo Alto, California.

Marquardt, M. & Kearsley, G. (1999), *Technology-based Learning*, St Lucie Press, Boca Raton.

Martin, R. (2003), 'Reporting the triple bottom line', *Human Capital*, March, pp. 6–10.

Medical Journal of Australia (2001), 'Sphere: A national depression project', *Medical Journal of Australia*, 175, 16 July.

Moullakis, J. (2003), 'CEOs "out of touch" with staff', *Australian Financial Review*, 7 March, p. 21.

Moxley, R. (1999), *Leadership and Spirit*, Jossey-Bass, San Francisco.

Needham, K. (2002), 'Abandon cult of early retirement. Howard urges', *Sydney Morning Herald*, 22 November, p. 2.

Neilson, G., Pasternack, B. & Viscio, A. (2000), 'Up the (E) organization', *Strategy and Business*, 18, pp. 52–61.

New South Wales Legal Information Access Centre (2001), *Hot Topics 32: E-law*, State Library of NSW, Sydney.

New Zealand Management (2001), 'Switching on to knowledge', *New Zealand Management*, May, pp. 42–6.

Newell, F. (2000), *Loyalty.com*, McGraw-Hill, New York.

Nicholson, N. (1998), 'How hardwired is human behaviour?', *Harvard Business Review*, July–August, pp. 135–47.

Nixon, S. (2002a), 'Bosses told to stamp out bullies', *Sydney Morning Herald*, 22 November.

—— (2002b), 'Call centre staff say their health is on the line, *Sydney Morning Herald*, 23–24 November, p. 7.

Nunn, K. (1996), 'Personal hopefulness: A conceptual review of the relevance of the perceived future to psychiatry', *British Journal of Medical Psychology*, 69, pp. 227–45.

Overhol, A., 'Virtually there?', *Fast Company*, 56, March 2002, pp. 108–14.

Owen, H. (2000), *The Power of Spirit*, Berrett-Koehler, San Francisco.

Pawle, F. (2002), 'Don Tapscott', *Australian Financial Review Boss Magazine*, 2 February, pp. 22–4.

Phillips, J. (1997), *Accountability in Human Resource Management*, Gulf Publishing, Houston.

Phillips, J. & Bonner, D. (2000), *Leading Knowledge Management and Learning*, ASTD, Alexandria, VA.

Pitis, S. (2001), 'Working longer and hating it', *The Australian*, 14 August, p. 4.

Pritchard, B. (2000), 'Narrow minds vs the big picture', *Marketing and eBusiness*, June, pp. 3–34.

Restak, R. (2000), *Mysteries of the Mind*, National Geographic, Washington DC.

Rollo, C. & Clarke, T. (2001), *International Best Practice—Case studies in knowledge management*, Standards Australia, Sydney.

Rosenberg, M. (2001), *e-Learning*, McGraw-Hill, New York.

Rosenfield, J. (2000), '5 trends to rock the world', *Marketing and eBusiness*, June, pp. 17–24.

—— (2001a), 'Customer focus-pocus', *Marketing and eBusiness*, June, pp. 15–19.

—— (2001b), 'Lies, damn lies and internet', *Marketing and eBusiness*, November, pp. 40–2.

Rylatt, A. D. (1997), *Navigating The Frenzied World of Work: The complete survival guide*, Business & Professional Publishing, Sydney.

—— (1999a), 'Why do our titanic ideas get sunk', *HR Monthly*, Australian Human Resources Institute, July, pp. 30–3.

—— (1999b), 'Creating high quality knowledge work', *Training and Development in Australia*, August, pp. 9–10.

—— (1999c), 'Building communities in your workplace', *Training Today—Members' newsletter*, Australian Institute of Training and Development, October, pp. 6–7.

—— (1999d), 'Workplace learning: A new box and dice', *People and Performance*, New Zealand Association for Training and Development, 6, 5, pp. 25–7.

—— (2000a), *Learning Unlimited: Practical strategies for transforming learning in the workplace of the 21st Century*, 2nd edn, Business + Publishing, Sydney.

—— (2000b), 'Putting knowledge to work: Changing the learning DNA in your workplace', *Training and Development*, December, pp. 4–8.

—— (2001), 'Desire to learn is the life force', *People and Performance*, February, pp. 20–6.

—— (2002), 'Editorial: Attracting and keeping talent: Nursing recruitment and selection', *Contemporary Nurse*, 13, 2–3, October, pp. 113–16.

Rylatt, A. D. & Lohan, K. (1995), *Creating Training Miracles*, Prentice Hall Australia, Sydney.

Sanchez, R. (2001), 'Managing knowledge into competence: The five learning cycles of the competent organization', keynote address at the fifth European International Design Management Conference, Amsterdam, 18–20 March.

Scott, R. (2000), 'A new line on on-line courses', *Sydney Morning Herald*, 26 April, p. 22.

Senge, P. M. (ed.) (1999), *The Dance of Change*, Nicholas Brealey Publishing, London.

Senge, P. M. & Carstedt, G. (2001), 'Innovating our way to the next industrial revolution', *MIT Sloan Management Review*, Winter, pp. 24–38.

Shackelford, B. (2002), 'A SCORM odyssey', *T + D*, August, pp. 30–5.

Silverman, G. (2001), *The Secrets of Word-of-mouth Marketing*, AMACOM, New York.

Slowman, M. (2001), 'The state of the e nation', *T + D*, August, pp. 61–2.

Slywotzky, A. J. & Morrison, D. J. (1998), *The Profit Zone: How strategic business design will lead you to tomorrow's profits*, Allen & Unwin, Sydney.

Sobel, D. (1995), *Longitude*, Fourth Estate, London.

St Vincent de Paul Society (2001), *A Long Road to Recovery*, St Vincent de Paul Society, Sydney.

Standards Australia (2001), *Knowledge Management: A framework for succeeding in the knowledge era*, Standards Australia, Sydney.

Stewart, T. (2001), *The Wealth of Knowledge*, Nicholas Brealey Publishing, London.

Sunderland, K. (2001), 'Portal power', *HR Monthly*, August, pp. 18–26.

Sveiby, K. E. (1997), *The New Organizational Wealth*, Berrett-Koehler, San Francisco.

Sydney Morning Herald (2002), 'Good reputation index', *Sydney Morning Herald*, 28 October, supplement.

Tanquist, S. (2001), 'Marathon e-learning', *T + D*, August, pp. 22–4.

Trincia, H. & Pawle, F. (2002), 'Knowledge management: Who's making it work? Case studies and interviews', *Australian Financial Review Boss Magazine*, 2 February, pp. 48–59.

Trout, J. & Rivhin, S. (1996), *The New Positioning*, McGraw-Hill, New York.

Upton, W. S. Jr (2001), *Business and Financial Reporting: Challenges from the new economy*, Financial Accounting Standards Board, Norwalk, Connecticut.

Urdan, T. & Weggen, C. (2000), *Corporate e-learning: Exploring a new frontier*, WR Hambrecht and Co., San Francisco.

Van Brakel, R. (2002), 'Why ROI isn't enough', *T + D*, June, pp. 72–4.

Van Buren, M. & Erskine, W. (2002), *State of the Industry Report 2002*, American Society for Training and Development, Alexandria, VA.

Vines, H. (2002), 'Survival Inc.', *HR Monthly*, February, pp. 14–16.

Watts, A. (1966), *The Book On The Taboo Against Knowing Who You Are*, Vintage Books, New York.

Wells, S. (1997), 'Building trust', *Executive Excellence*, September, p. 11.

Wenger, E. C. & Snyder, W. M. (2000), 'Communities of practice: The organizational frontier', *Harvard Business Review*, January–February, pp. 139–45.

West, C. (2001), *Competitive Intelligence*, Palgrave, Houndhills, UK.

Wheatley, M. J. & Kellner-Rogers, M. (1996), *A Simpler Way*, Berrett-Koehler, San Francisco.

Williams, M. (2001), 'CRM promises and disasters in 2000', *Marketing and eBusiness*, December–January, pp. 40–1.

Woodhouse, M. (2002), 'Loyal is not a verb', *Marketing and eBusiness*, June, pp. 49–50.

Work and Family Unit (2001), *Balancing the Till in 2000: Finding and keeping good people in the retail sector*, Work and Family Unit, Canberra.

Zemke, R., Raines, C. & Filipczak, B. (2000), *Generations at Work*, AMACOM, New York.

Zenger, J. & Uehlein, C. (2001), 'Why blended will win', *T + D*, August, pp. 54–60.

Web references

www.accountability.org.uk   for AccountAbility, the Institute of Social and Ethical AccountAbility

www.actu.asn.au   for a site full of research and studies on worker issues by the Australian Council of Trade Unions

www.adlnet.org   for information on Advanced Distribution Learning network (ADL network) and a more detailed exploration of advances in e-learning (e.g. SCORM)

www.alastairrylatt.com   for Alastair Rylatt Consulting and the Workplace Learning Help Desk, free resources and many more links

www.att.com/learningnetwork   for the AT&T Learning Network, which has a wide range of on-line learning resources

www.BotSpot.com   an Internet clearinghouse for bots and intelligent agents

www.brandon-hall.com   a site rich in web-based learning, this is Brandon Hall's site

www.brint.com   an extensive portal on knowledge management

www.bsr.org   for excellent resources and the latest worldwide news in the field of business and social responsibility, this is the Business for Social Responsibility site

www.businessexcellence.co.nz a site responsible for business excellence
accreditation and awards in New Zealand

www.cio.com/forums/knowledge for CIO magazine's focus on
knowledge management issues with extensive links to other sites, visit
the CIO's Knowledge Management Research Center site

www.cisco.com for whitepapers and pointers on digital technology,
e-learning and implementation, visit Cisco Systems' site

www.collaboration-tools.com for a wonderful gateway to the latest
advances in collaborative technology, visit the Collaboration and
Knowledge Management Resource Center's site

www.copyright.org.au for the Australian Copyright Council and the
latest resources in this important field

www.disastercenter.com/copyrite.htm a useful listing of articles on
copyright and intellectual property, with links

www.ecosustainable.com.au/links.htm#7 provides information on
environmental sustainability in business and a portal of immense value

www.edna.edu.au for an Australian gateway to resources and services for
education and training

www.epss.com an extensive portal devoted to performance support and
knowledge management

www.fasb.org provides information about accounting standards; this is
the Financial Accounting Standards Board's site

www.globalreporting.org for information about the Global Reporting
Initiative (GRI)

www.hrinz.org.nz for an excellent gateway to human resources
discussions, and a great links page, visit the Human Resources Institute
of New Zealand's site

www.iacmp.org for the International Association of Career Management
Professionals' reports on career trends and support

www.iasb.org.uk for the latest on the accounting profession and an
introduction to International Standards for combined accounts,
including both tangible and intangible assets

www.icasit.org/km a general site on knowledge management

www.idc.com for a very popular site on the latest in the information and
knowledge economy, visit IDC's site

www.informationweek.com a great way to keep up to date on digital
technology and explore knowledge-alert updates on topics of interest

www.ipaustralia.gov.au for resources on protecting intellectual property,
visit Intellectual Property Australia's site

www.istart.co.nz an excellent New Zealand portal on IT news and
business digital innovation

www.keepem.com   an excellent starting point for study in the staff retention field

www.knowledge.standards.com.au   for the Standards Australia knowledge management study group

www.law.gov.au/publications   for resources on law and intellectual property, and the selected publications of the Attorney-General's Department

www.law.monash.edu.au/clide   provides some excellent resources and links on e-law; this is the Centre for Law in the Digital Economy (CLIDE) site

www.learningcircuits.org   an e-learning site by the American Society for Training & Development

www.masie.com   the Masie Center's hub for e-learning

www.netconference.about.com   covers Internet conferencing, instant messaging, videoconferencing, webcam and more, and is a good site for keeping up to date in this emerging field

www.noie.gov.au   for the National Office for the Information Economy (an Australian government resource)

www.nzbcsd.org.nz   for a hub for sustainable development and case study examples, visit the New Zealand Business Council for Sustainable Development's site

www.onap.fsu.edu   the site of the Office for Needs Assessment and Planning

www.oznetlaw.net   for a site providing information on Internet and e-commerce, visit the Communications Law Centre's site

www.scip.org   for a gateway to resources and networking in the field of competitive intelligence, visit the Society of Competitive Intelligence Professionals' site

www.searchtools.com   a site full of resources for business applications of search facilities

www.standardsinstitute.org   for the site of the International Intangible Management Standards Institute

www.stevedenning.com   a site that discusses the use of story in communicating change

www.sveiby.com   for a site that explores measuring intangible assets, visit the Sveiby Knowledge Management site

www.w3.org   for a clearinghouse of conversations on standards and protocols for the Internet, visit the World Wide Web Consortium's site

www.wipo.org   an excellent site of global trends on copyright and intellectual property of the World Intellectual Property Organization (WIPO)

www.workplace.gov.au/WorkFamily   an excellent starting place for work–family friendly implementation in business, this is the Australian Workplace portal

Index